THE

BARTLETT

MArch
GAD

GRADUATE
ARCHITECTURAL
DESIGN

2011 / 2012

INTRODUCTION

The MArch Graduate Architecture Design (GAD) is a one-year postgraduate course, conceived to provide open access to advanced research in architecture, and is open to all, internationally.

The first phase of the complete re-design of the postgraduate programme will offer the MArch Urban Design and the MArch GAD, both of which will be installed in the new building — the Royal Ear Hospital — providing a more visible entity devoted to prospective architecture. Once realised, the new overarching scheme will become known as 'B.PRO'. It will offer more structured access to the realisation and application of research and the production of new schemes of conception and construction in architecture and urbanism.

To this end, the 2011-2012 MArch GAD was organised around six 'research clusters'. These clusters featured more specific research in a number of domains, and offered the opportunity to gain access to new computational tools and a new culture of scripting, directly connected to tools of fabrication. Inspired by and directly related to the current scene of international architecture creation, the teaching of software packages such as Maya, Arduino and other processing platforms are all taught from the perspective of an innovative idea of conception and fabrication.

The Bartlett International Lecture Series presented the opportunity for students to be confronted by the main streams of research that will be influential in the near future. Through the different critical sessions, it was possible to enjoy the process of evolution in the work of the students; the final exhibition with the presentation of drawings, models and animations, all of a very high quality, is clearly demonstrative of the intense activity undertaken throughout the year.

Whether produced through groups or conducted as individual research, all the work demonstrates an incredible energy and a richness which reveals a very large diversity of approaches enriched by cultural and individual experience and interests.

As an international course with students who come from all over the world, and with the field trips (to destinations such as Reykjavik, New York, Berlin and Austria) MArch GAD gives the students the chance to discover new realities — and their attendant possible contextual implications. Through the federative idea of creative architecture, the MArch GAD is the opportunity to find a way to participate in a new community but also to affirm the singularity and the originality of individual talents.

This twelve-month course is not only an open door to advanced architecture but also the base from which to define a singular practice and for each student to invent a strategy to find a position in the professional world.

The September 2012 MArch GAD exhibition and this catalogue provide an excellent overview of the depth of quality and the intensity of the teaching of the Bartlett's tutors. What it also showcases is the passion of all the students involved in the programme.

Frederic Migayrou
Bartlett Professor of Architecture
Director of B.PRO

Contents

fletcher priest architects
trust

MArch GAD
External Examiners

Matias del Campo
DTMA — SIVA Fudan University,
SPAN Architecture & Design

Evan Douglis
Rensselaer Polytechnic Institute,
Evan Douglis Studio

Kas Oosterhuis
TU Delft,
ONL [Oosterhuis_Lénárd]

Luca Galofaro
IaN+

MArch GAD

RESEARCH CLUSTER

1

INCREASED RESOLUTION FABRIC OF ARCHITECTURE

Alisa Andrasek, Jose Sanchez

RC1 explored openings within emergent modes of production at various scales for instances of the higher resolution fabrics of architecture. Given architecture's nascent tendency to generate legible synthesis, it has the potential to play an important role in the accelerated convergence of matter and information. While data visualisation exposes the hidden beauty, intelligence, and complexity of observed systems, data materialisation can produce such beauty and complexity within new synthetic fields. In order to develop such data materialisation processes, it is necessary to descend to the finer grains of computational building blocks, where the design search is performed within constellations of billions of particles. The power of many small, decentralised agents within simulations and generative methods is enabling the capture of complexity and nontrivial synthesis within design systems, which are resistant to linear decomposition. Discretisation in the domain of computational logics and algorithmic structure can now be extended to the domain of matter and newly accessible building blocks for synthetic material formations. The found physics of complex material processes, such as massive-scale erosion and sedimentation or ice melting, can now be encapsulated through computational physics and large data sets, embedded into simulations and, consequently, physical construction.

Expanding discoveries in material science are now being incorporated through simulation into massive resolution design speculations across various scales, opening doors for weird syntheses and fissuring established preconceptions of what architecture could be. Architects can go beyond geometry to directly design the structure of matter itself.

Building blocks of computational design ecology are descending to the primordial soup of logics, towards distributed information processing rather than centralised procedural formats, resulting in more resilience. Such computational models are coming closer to the way information is processed in living organisms. Instead of centralised linear functions, there is a prevalence of distributed discrete neighborhood based computing. Apart from the nature of information transfer, likeness to biology is increasing on the level of complex performance of architecture. With living organisms, distribution of energy and nutrients literally happens through bodies, as high-resolution vessels for such flows. Built fabrics of increased resolution have potential to come closer to such models, whereby architecture becomes direct vessel for energy production and its fibres reach higher levels of performance.

Such an architecture is drawing upon large data from the finer-grain physics of matter — matter as information enabled by computation. Matter acquires active agency in the process of becoming instead of being treated as a passive design ingredient. There is greater designability in the algorithmic profiles of matter, since computational simulations can absorb large data from real contexts and provide access to the underlying code of matter. This not only expands technically enriched material formations, but also activates previously hidden material powers toward designs beyond our anticipation in both formal imagination and performance.

Since computational kernel processes are built on porous boundaries between systems, the economic flow of production could also be engaged within the fibres of generative processes, allowing design to evolve within production fitness. The RC1 research was initiated with a brief design challenge sponsored by Unilever, synthesising data collected with Kinect (low resolution motion sensing 3D camera) with Multi-Agent based behaviors (scripted in Processing). It engaged the idea of "unnatural" or exaggerated materiality through design of visual effects — achieved through computational physics. Expressive movements of (human) actors (from The Royal Ballet) were recorded at different speeds and resolution. Collected point clouds were than a "host" condition for different computational entities to be spawn from. Supernatural enhancements to the movement, synthetic physics of liquids, concepts such as viscosity, elasticity, and density were unfolded through computational matter. Coordination of temporal sequencing of different processes and resolutions was studied, allowing for unnatural speeds (via computational time) to be mined for counter-intuitive aesthetics.

Teams of students then engaged research on particular ecologies of production, such as additive manufacturing (3D printing), harnessing of computational physics for simulation of air flows as agency in construction of complex shell structures, re-designing construction site based on distributed robotic swarms, to mention a few. By developing architecture of a whole design ecology — including physics of matter at fine grain, logics of production protocols, generative constructability behaviors in synthesis with design intent, each student team developed a pilot design proposal mining the potency of new kind of materiality and often counter-intuitive aesthetics spawning from it. Found natural physics of light or air were amplified, machines acquired designer behaviors, architectural fabrics with higher resolution were tested in myriad speculative scenarios. The cluster explored both technologically advanced and computationally cutting edge territories and simultaneously sophisticated, fresh and counter-intuitive aesthetics.

RC1 Students: Wei Chang, Vincenzo D'Auria, Tingwei Duan, Alberto Fernandez Gonzalez, Nicolo Friedman, Hoang Le Minh, Mark Muscat, Xueying Pang, Pallavi Sharma, Chuti Sringuanvilas, Shuliang Wang, Lingdong Zeng, Mingyu Zhu, Li Zhu

Chuti Sringuanvilas, Shuliang Wang, Lingdong Zeng, 'Flow Catcher' was a design research project that started with the question of how to capture fluid vector quality, such as velocity and direction, and transform it to architectural fabric. In reality, fluid particles are invisible unless there is an additional material. The process of the research started with material experiments to study physics properties between airflow and material geometry, and brought material behaviour properties into a computational simulation process. At the end of the research, the system was transformed into an inhabitable architectural proposal by a fabrication process, to capture air turbulence with simple lightweight geometries. **Fig. 1.1** Combined modular scenario in fabrication system. **Fig. 1.2** A cross-section showing complexity of fluid vector field in an inhabitable space. **Fig. 1.3** A physical model created from the setup of inputting material into a simple shape container to capture air turbulence. This setup had been used through out the entire research. **Fig. 1.4** An interior rendering of an inhabitable structure, with geometries entangled together to create architectural fabric. **Fig. 1.5 — 1.6** With transportation consideration, each module was restricted to the size of 2.4 x 12 x 4.5 metres (width x length x height), and assembled together to create a house. **Fig. 1.7** Storm-like formation that was created from air-pressure nozzles arranged in computational simulation.

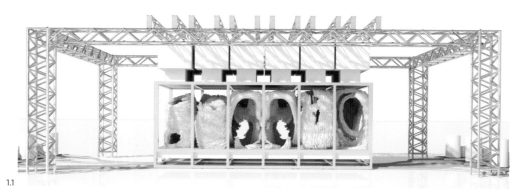

1.1

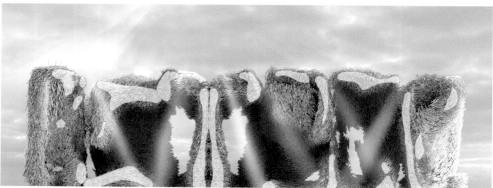

1.2

1.3

1.4

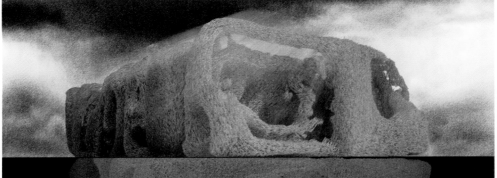

1.5

1.6

1.7

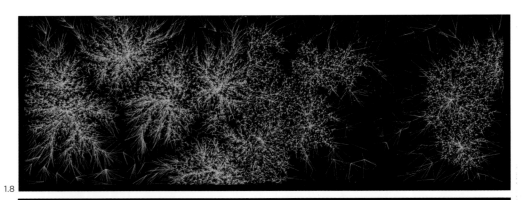

1.8

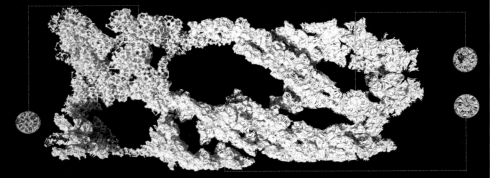

1.9

1.10

Mingyu Zhu, Wei Chang, Tingwei Duan, 'Ghost Writer' is a system developed for generating an intelligent mould for casting glass in sequences of cells, which can improve the lighting environment in architecture. **Fig. 1.8** Inspired by nature, the ghost system can generate certain forms with algorithms derived from the complex growth logic of plants and organisms. **Fig. 1.9 — 1.10** Each ghost cell can be replaced by a different cell, according to a predetermined sequence. **Fig. 1.11** The Ghost Writer system is a tool for designing the moulds for casting glass as well as structures for architecture. In order to enhance the diversity of the glass fabrication and to increase different optical effects such as distortion, dispersion, and caustic effect in real architecture, the nonlinear behaviour of melting glass is simulated and used for controlling the form of the three-dimensional glass. **Fig. 1.12** This new fabrication method is used to create a Museum of Light in Iceland with an intricate lighting environment. The Museum can offer different kinds of light experience such as delicate reflection and distortion, complex shadow and caustic effects.

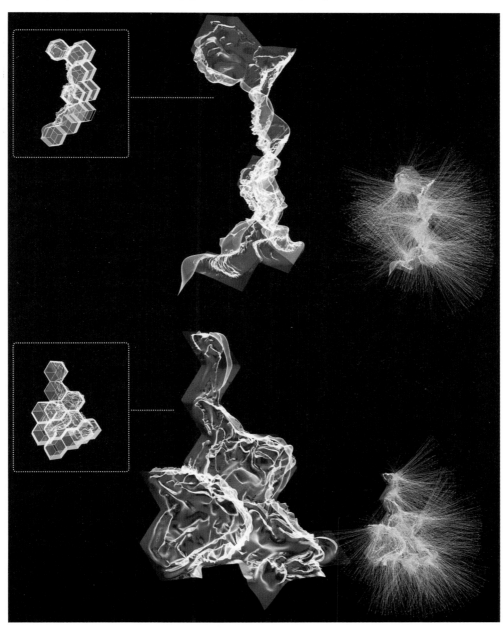

Fig. 1.13 Alberto Fernández, 'Recurv/e/sive'. Architecture as memory device can navigate over the accumulated data from residual spaces, generating an organic growing answer as layering structure. This growing logic can be adaptive in more complex scenarios due to its high density based on a grid of 20 x 20 x 20 cm. **Fig. 1.14** Building the hidden data field generated in the urban landscape, translating the information as points, lines and curves. As a result, it is possible to obtain structures that can grow in the available urban voids. **Fig 1.15** New urban facilities as generative folies in the urban tissue, designing conditions more than rigid spaces. **Fig 1.16** Generative robot using discrete movements (based on crystal growing simulations) can translate the initial data field in a spaceframe as urban micro scaffolding, over which it is possible to regenerate the existent fabric, treading the recursive memory path with 3 different shapes. **Fig 1.17** Structural continuity treading the existent framework. The system works as a continuous reinforcement, redistributing the forces in the whole structure, defining columns, beams, walls and floors by density of this memory paths.

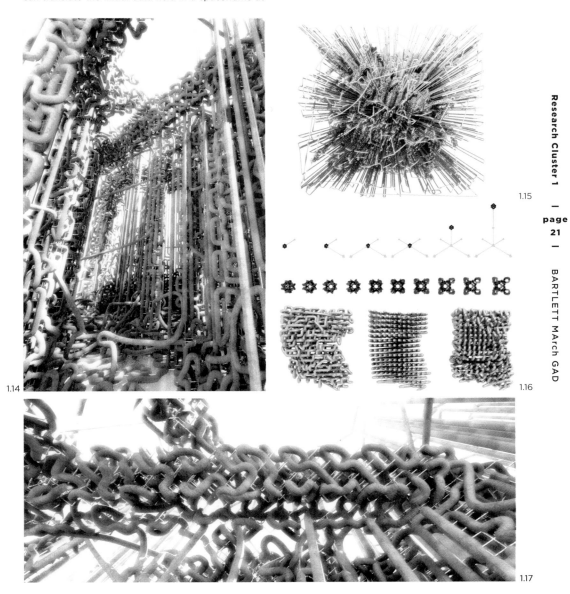

1.14

1.15

1.16

1.17

Le Minh Hoang, Xueying Pang, 'Reloading'. This project focuses mainly on self-assemble and high-resolution architecture. We consider architecture as a living object, specifically, it could change or transform, interacting with the outside environment. The idea of lattice structure from crystal and the work of agents has also been researched to support the main concept. In this project, robots have been a considerably useful tools in developing the whole concept. Robots could not only be highly compatible with the codes, relating to agents or lattice structures, but also a practical way to build up architecture in reality. This system has been used in a specific area on the Sendai seashore, which suffers many tsunamis every year. The system offered a specific building, constructed by robots, which could be automatically transformed to be adaptive to the environment there, preventing people from experiencing natural disasters. Although there could be arguments for this, this system could be a recommended method to build up our living environment. **Fig. 1.18** The project proposes a kind of living architecture, which duplicates the natural properties such as composing, decomposing and recomposing items into a robotic ecology. Based on the self-organisation system (agent system), the buildings have the ability to be adaptive to their environment. **Fig. 1.19** The digital simulation of the robot system collaborates with the agent system and adapts to the geography. **Fig. 1.20** The bird's eye view overall. **Fig. 1.21** The internal view of the building. The outstretched part of the building. **Fig. 1.22** Detail of the robotically constructed structural fabric.

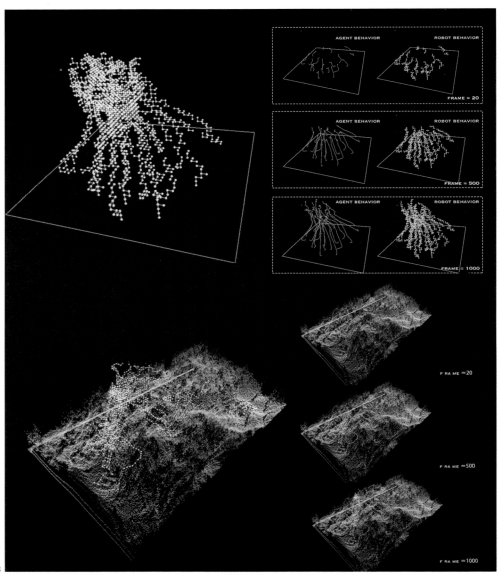

1.18

1.20

1.21

1.22

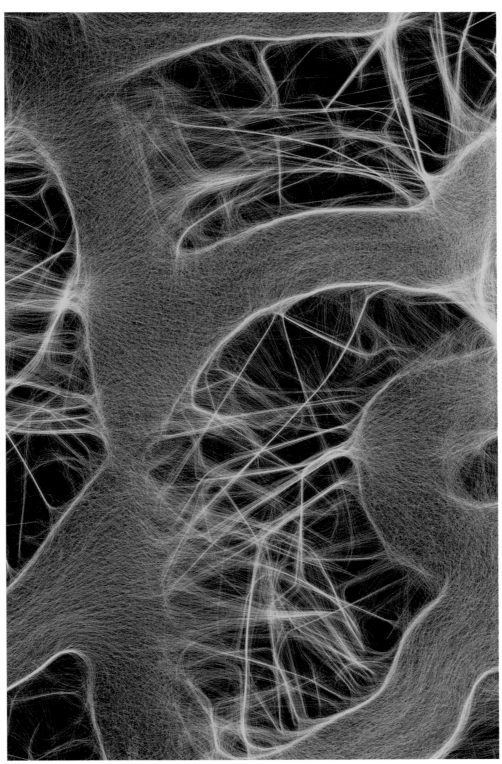

1.23

Team Variance: Vincenzo D'Auria, Nicolò Friedman, Mark Geoffrey Muscat, Pallavi Sharma. 'nDprint: On a global scale', a form is developed using a Reaction-Diffusion algorithm by controlling distribution of matter in space with applied fitness conditions of housing topology and structure. Engaging agents that generate fibrous distribution of matter producing performance within the fabric, imbue the form with materiality on a micro scale. These digital formations are materialised by modes of additive manufacturing. The aim of this project is to propose an architectural fabric which is responsive towards its surroundings. It is not blocking or fighting back applied pressures, but it is withstanding and adapting towards them. With design, structures, construction and material technologies interacting within themselves, our fabric

acquired a higher resolution in terms of its performance, design and existence. **Fig. 1.23** Data-maps are generated using RD system, which are analysed by agents depending on the luminosity of each data-cell. Agents perform behaviours corresponding to luminosity range, and create matter distribution performative patterns. **Fig. 1.24** Detail 1: The Internal composition of spaces is given the behaviour to add texture to the space. Compact, entangled fibres provide sufficient rigidity to the partitions while the drooping fibres provide a soft and tangible, hair-like texture. **Fig. 1.25** Detail 2: This behaviour corresponds to the outlying and foremost part of the fabric. This is the major transition zone of energies between natural and built environment. The first behaviour is very compact, entangled fibrous distribution aiming to lock air inside in

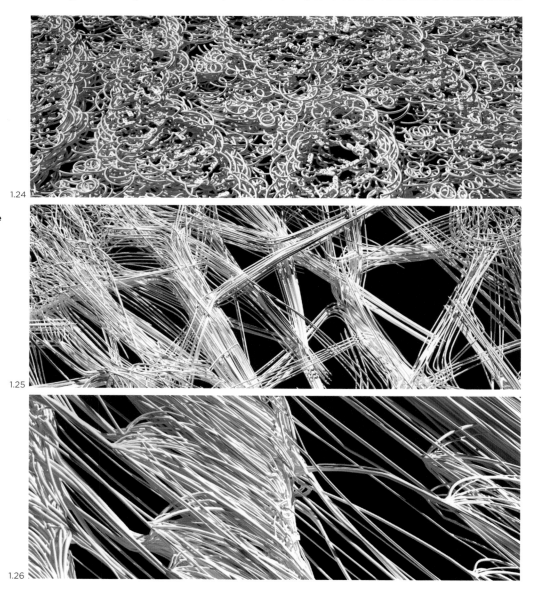

1.24

1.25

1.26

order to facilitate thermal insulation. On the other hand, the second behaviour is more open and has independent distribution, to provide maximum exposure to sunlight as these fibres are intended to be printed with photoluminescent material. **Fig. 1.26** Detail 3: When the fabric begins to span, the behaviour mutates into rigid alignment, regularly coiling into cohesive bundles and pushing its tensile properties. **Fig. 1.27 — 1.29** Housing typology is chosen to obtain a particular fitness condition and a global scale to proposed architectural fabric. This in turn also forms the basis for design and for distribution and organisation of matter in the fabric. Agency logic keeps this continuity through re-organisation of the fibres, and generates performance depending on their distribution.

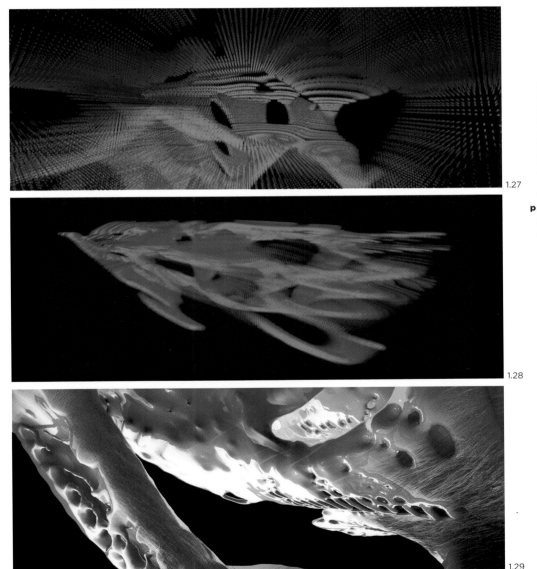

1.27

1.28

1.29

1.30

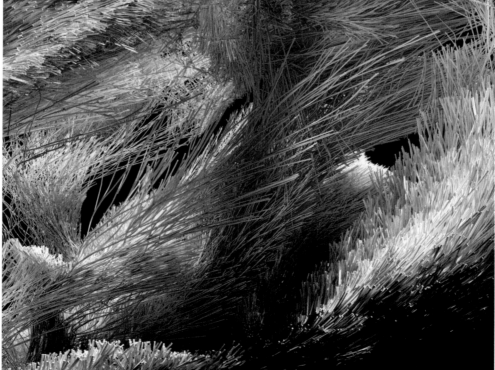

1.31

Fig. 1.30 MakerBot Replicator is a dual extrusion 3D printer that gave us the opportunity to test the materiality of our fabric. These 3D prints are the results of digitally generated materiality intertwining with different settings of printer, which adds to digital possibilities. For example, calibrating the nozzle speed of the machine and feed rate of the material hence creating spongy deposition. **Fig. 1.31** Three-dimensional agency growth within the reaction diffusion voxel. **Fig. 1.32 — 1.33** Agents are introduced into the three-dimensional reaction diffusion data map to create a global-scale fibrous distribution. Agent trails are identified by a different colour denoting their length and in turn their strength. Red denotes strongest fibres while blue denotes the weakest ones.

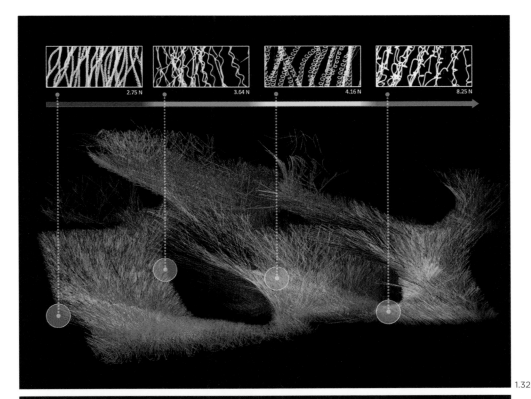

1.32

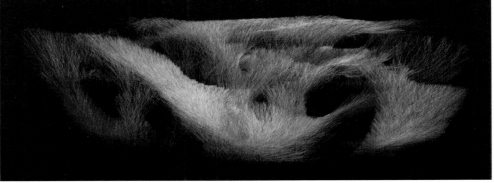

1.33

The Northern Lights are sighted during RC1's Field Trip to Iceland

RC1 External Examination (left to right: Luca Galofaro, Frédéric Migayrou, Daniel Widrig,
Alisa Andrasek, Ilona Lenard, Kas Oosterhuis., Evan Douglis , Matias del Campo)

RC1 Field Trip to Iceland

MArch GAD Crits (left to right: Xavier de Kestelier, Andrew Porter, Stephen Gage, Frédéric Migayrou)

MArch GAD crits (left to right: Marjan Colletti, Daniel Widrig, Fulvio Wirz, Frédéric Migayrou)

RC1 Field Trip to Iceland

MArch GAD

RESEARCH CLUSTER

2

FORM FOLLOWS FETISH

Marjan Colletti, Guan Lee, Tea Lim

Louis Sullivan's dictum *Form follows Function* is certainly one of the most known and also misunderstood statements in architectural history. Falsely propagated as a diktat against ornamentation and in favour of functionalism, yet seemingly still in vogue. RC2 accepts the presence, experience and body of architecture as a given and often underestimated fact. The premise was that form is here to stay because it may well be the primary, and also ultimate, asset of architecture.

First of all it must be said that most often form outlives function. Many buildings perform other, different functions than originally planned for because it has become obsolete, or because the program has evolved so much that it had to move out, due to change in size, politics, finances or performance. Secondly, the proliferation of digital techniques has brought a close to the seemingly enduring separation of function and ornamentation in architecture. Whether sculpted, 3D scanned, simulated or scripted — this was of no importance to RC2 this year — small variations in software protocols and fabrication mechanics can result in the more or less exuberant articulation of ornate surfaces and volumes. Therefore, it would be fair to say that it is form that should ideally be more controlled and planned by architects than function (as a description of required performance) to have more chances to survive societal change, and that it is function that has long lost its primacy as design purpose, scope and object(ivity) over, for example, complex, texturised geometric formations.

With *Form follows Fetish* students were asked to formulate powerful individual sets of values for design rather than generic criteria. Each individual process is defined by strong aesthetic principles (related to objects, materials) and intrinsic psychological factors (analyzing behaviours, fixations). We understood fetish(isation) in architecture as an extremely precise articulation of aspired perfection — albeit usually exaggerated, even dysmorphic — and/or gratification — albeit often obsessive and compulsive. That we found it truly contemporary is partly due to the revived architectural discourse on beauty++ and nature 2.0, but also due to novel design and fabrication aestheticisation processes, protocols and rituals. A further advantage that the concept of fetish appeared to us is that it also raises questions on ethnicity, religion, sexuality, underground culture, and thus provides an alternative argument on architectural design that is not bound within stylistic globalisation or standardised design methodologies — possibly the necessary framework for a truly international programme such as the MArch GAD.

RC2 is a *research by design* cluster. Perhaps a set phrase, but in truth mostly reversed into design by research: i.e. where form follows software, programme. Instead, we embarked on the dangerous endeavour of focusing less on process, but more on *practice*. In fact, at least half of the work was produced in a workshop/factory (Grymsdyke Farm). RC2 familiarizes students not only with digital drafting techniques, but more importantly with the expertise of digital crafting. Those toolsets, which are required to run a CNC machine or prepare files appropriately for 3D Rapid Prototyping of extreme models are in some sense *invisible* skills. They cannot be documented in portfolio sheets, they reveal themselves in the output itself. We may call these: digital craft.

Consequently, in accordance to the quest of practice as part of the yearly brief, in January, February and March we designed and fabricated a large installation: *aRC(2)himera*. It was installed at the Haus der Architektur in Graz Austria as part of the group exhibition *By all means — analogue/digital experimental settings* (29.03. — 11.05.2012) together with the TU Graz and the Academy of Fine Arts Vienna. The *aRC(2)himera* is an architectural chimera. From its distinct sets of digital chromosomes and analogue chromosomes evolved a monstrous mix-up of various approaches that went from developing skin morphologies, structure anatomies, ornamental textures, coral growth scripts, steampunk aesthetics, flocking simulations etc. To some this may look and sound outrageous and horrific — as it is neither elegant nor pure, nor truthful or correct (process-wise). To us, such Frankensteinian, modern Promethean approach and the elegant grotesqueness of the piece are only relative. As a digital-analogue hybrid, it must be seen in a context of post-digital synthesis, hybridity and new potentialities. Fully digitally designed and fabricated, it was assembled by the students by hand: 600 CNC milled foam triangles, 350 rubber bands, 20 laser-cut Perspex pieces, 1200 laser-cut Perspex joints 14400 metal pins.

The aims of such an exercise were clear. Firstly, students should experience the difficulty of translating a digital model into a larger prototype with joints, gravity and material parameters. Secondly, invoking the feeling of achievement that real physical output gives as compared to on-screen research. And thirdly, generating a sense of confidence in each student: if they managed to build an installation with software tools and fabrication technologies new to them, surely they could extrapolate a rich formal and contextual research process, detached from structural or programmatic functionalism and more defined by their own personal approach. Ergo, *Form follows Fetish*.

RC2 Students: Muhammad Hissan Awaiz Randhawa, Liang Cao, Vasilis Chlorokostas, Minsi Hu, Adamantia Keki, Cris Kuan-Yi Lee, Sahar Navabakhsh, Jing Shen, Yifan Tian, Le Zhai, Jingyi Zhou, Li Zhu, Sydney Zuellig

2.1

2.2a

2.2b

2.2c

2.2d

2.2e

2.2f

2.2g

2.2h

Fig. 2.1 'aRC(2)himera'. The finalised installation in the 'Mit Allen Mittlen' (By All Means) exhibition at the Haus der Architektur, Kunsthaus Graz on 29th March 2012. **Fig. 2.2** 'aRC(2)himera'. Collection of textures: **a.** Le Zhai, **b.** Vasilis Chlorokostas, **c.** Muhammad Hissaan Awaiz Randhawa, **d.** Jing Shen, **e.** Liang Cao, **f.** Adamantia Keki, **g.** Sydney Zuellig, **h.** Yifan Tian. **Fig. 2.3** 'aRC(2)himera'. 2-Dimensional Skinning map of the textures merging from one to another.

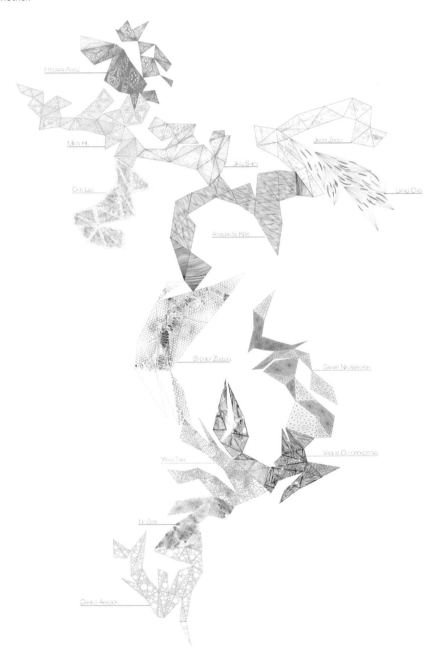

2.3

Fig. 2.4 Vasilis Chlorokostas, 'InfraSkin'. Various subdivision levels of the infraSkin. Manipulated CatmullClark subdivisions bridge the border between form and texture in search of scale. **Fig. 2.5** Vasilis Chlorokostas, 'InfraSkin'. Application of cavity specific transparency and colour, defining a new fractalised environment. Geometry subdivision is used as the architectural equivalent of cellular subdivision. The subdivisions that lead one cell to become an organism meet an architecture that starts from the object and progresses towards the atom.

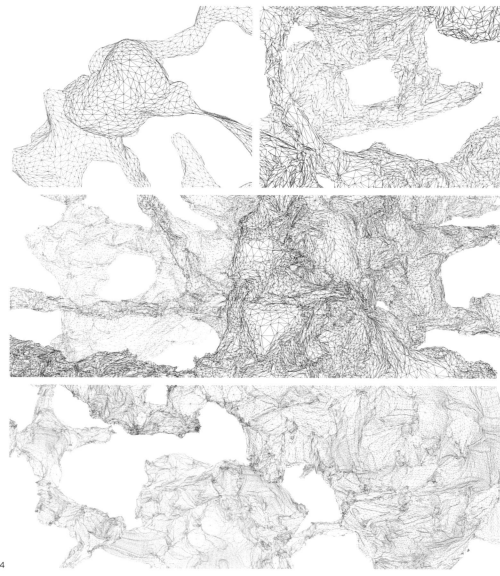

Fig. 2.6 Le Zhai, 'Nanosuit' Body Armour. Swarming Agents move around the suit to define personal region and control the iterations on the suit. **Fig. 2.7** Le Zhai, 'Swarming Space'. The implementation of swarm behaviour to aid the defining of space by tracking the trail of units, to be reflected on the base volume. Extended movement of the units with the result in a volumised definition. **Fig. 2.8** Adamantia Keki, 'From Fold to Wrinkle'. Fractal 1:investigation of the formation of an expression through mirror symmetry and repetition as a method of growth and expansion of a 3d meta-ball system applied on neutral point network. **Fig. 2.9** Adamantia Keki, 'From Fold to Wrinkle'. Ready: development of an expressive 3d meta-ball system on a neutral point network system affected by multiple attractors. **Fig. 2.10 — 2.11** Adamantia

Keki, 'From Fold to Wrinkle'. Cover: conceptual drawing investigating the erosion and evolution of facial expressions over time on multiple 3d meta-ball systems affected by multiple external and internal attractors, applied on 3d point networks.

2.6

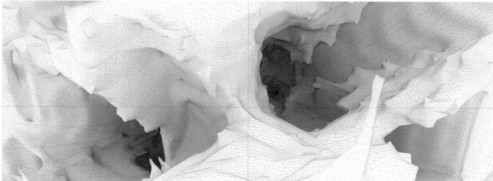

2.7

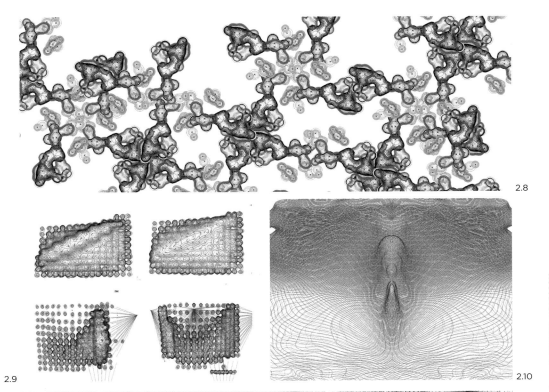

2.8

2.9

2.10

2.11

Fig. 2.12 Zhu Li, 'Digital Weaving'. Realization of methods woven together. **Fig. 2.13** Zhu Li, 'Digital Weaving'. Generating the process. **Fig. 2.14** Cris Lee, 'MIKE' (Mobile Interior: Kinetic Environment). The transformation of the car simulates a dynamic surface, attempting to achieve the goal to design a car with dynamic body. **Fig. 2.15** Cris Lee, 'MIKE'. Section illustrating the dynamic interface between with people, car and environment. **Fig. 2.16** Cris Lee, 'MIKE'. Staircases are transformed from traditional models via the use of Smart Form technology, providing a new approach and transformation for the design.

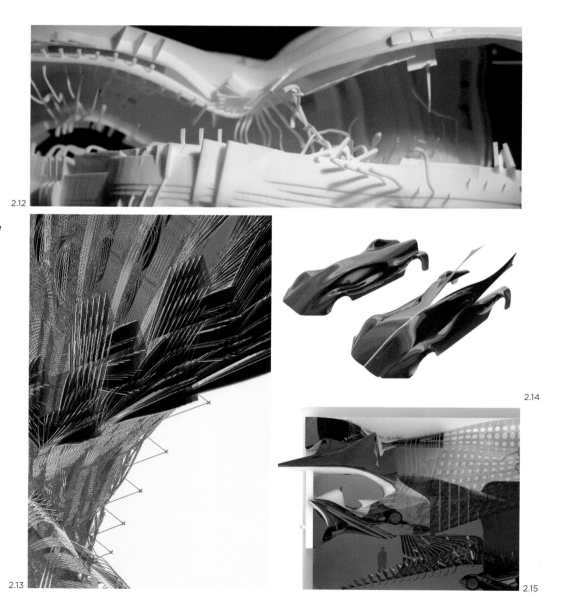

2.12

2.13

2.14

2.15

2.16

2.17

2.18

Fig. 2.17 Sahar Navabakhsh, 'Embodiment and the Imagery of Percept'. Stills from the animation simulating a story by J.G. Ballard, which shows generation and reformation of space through embodied experience and body interaction with a 'psychotropic' house, where the inhabitant becomes the interpreter of the environment by how it's imagined, perceived and in ways body, its movement and psychic attributes of mind are in dialogue with the domicile they encounter. **Fig. 2.18** Sahar Navabakhsh, 'Embodiment and the Imagery of Percept'. 99 Stellavista is a PT house where form follows fetish through perceptual figure-ground interaction and moods of its occupants; architectural opportunities arise from these imprints, affecting the existential spatial preconception. **Fig. 2.19 — 2.20** Sydney Zuellig, 'Obsessive Compulsive Design'. A home of organised chaos challenging the normals through the occupier's obsession with corners and spikes resulting in the corruption of order.

2.19

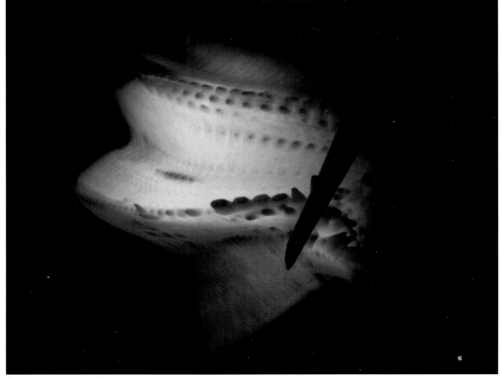

2..20

Fig. 2.21 Liang Cao, 'Metabolicity'. This is a rebuilding project of Euston station, London. Multiple platforms create a new station, satisfying an increasing traffic flow. Sunlight also reaches the lower ground level due to optimisation of the form of the platforms. There is an investigation into construction methods using the aid of robotics. Plan drawing of Euston Square Gardens. **Fig. 2.22** Liang Cao, 'Metabolicity'. Section drawing of Euston tube station. **Fig. 2.23** Liang Cao, 'Metabolicity'. Proposed construction process. **Fig. 2.24** Liang Cao, Metabolicity. Section drawing of Euston train station. **Fig. 2.25** Liang Cao, 'Metabolicity'. New Euston station under construction.

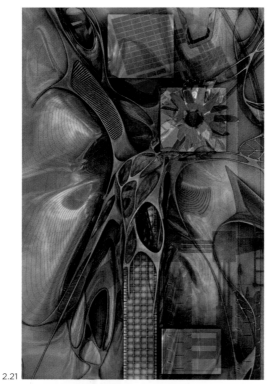

2.21

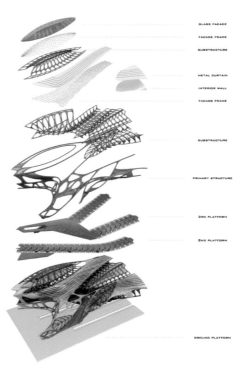

2.22

2.23

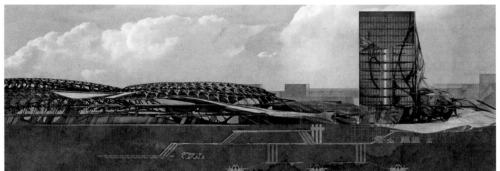

2.24

2.25

Fig. 2.26 Minsi Hu, Jing Shen, Yifan Tian, Jingyi Zhou, 'Fetish Garden'. A complex garden situated in an imaginary location, combining and merging the individual attributes of the personal fetishes of reflection, the sound of rustling leaves, mosaic tiling and nails. Underground texture and details: standing beneath a forest of diverse leaves. **Fig. 2.27** 'Fetish Garden'. Top view of the upper landscape: a series of magical layers. **Fig. 2.28** 'Fetish Garden'. Top view of the lake: beside the high grass, there is a calm lake in which the water has endless aftertastes. **Fig. 2.29** 'Fetish Garden'. The space up in the air consists of pieces of floating leave structures, in which birds may fly around and sing. **Fig. 2.30** 'Fetish Garden'. Detailed view of the landscape and floating leaves.

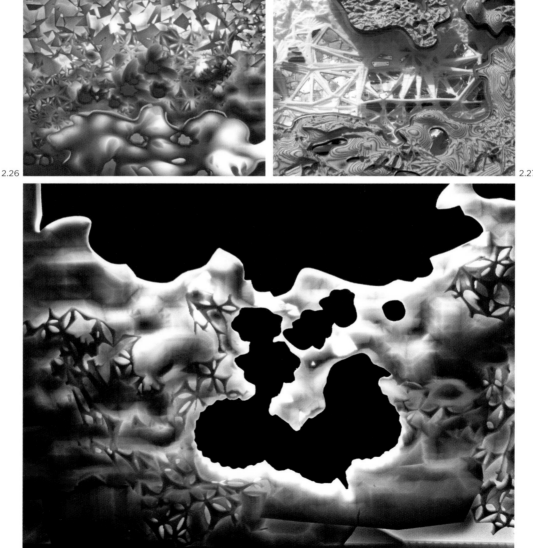

2.26

2.27

2.28

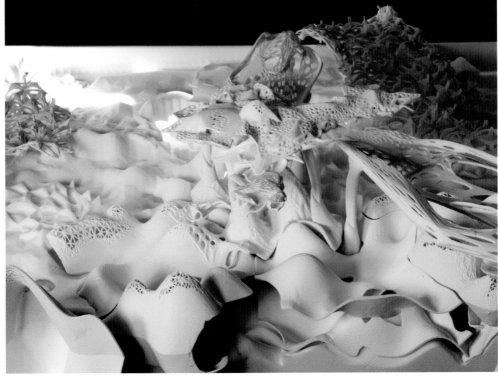

Fig. 2.31 — 2.33 Muhammad Hissaan Awaiz Randhawa, 'The Inhabitable Staircase'. A project that argues the conventional practice of designing spaces, volumes and ornaments as separate entities. By using human body (neck) M.R.I data as a tool and a methodology to design and to speculate architecture, the inhabitable staircase grows and deforms under the notion of disease (F.O.P) creating a new potentiality. **Fig. 2.34** Muhammad Hissaan Awaiz Randhawa, 'The Inhabitable Staircase.' The deformation of the staircase potentially develops new shading spaces, ornaments, and fenestration to be a part of architecture. Filamentous handrails deform into structural elements which spread to become canopies and these canopies deform to create ornament and fenestration. The project is a celebration of new potential spaces in architecture. **Fig. 2.35** Muhammad Hissaan Awaiz Randhawa, 'The Inhabitable Staircase'. The staircase deforms to create new inhabitable spaces as living pods, filaments and ornament all becoming a part of an overarching system in a constant flux. The staircase develops living pods as its extension due to the influence of disease, creating new architectural spaces.

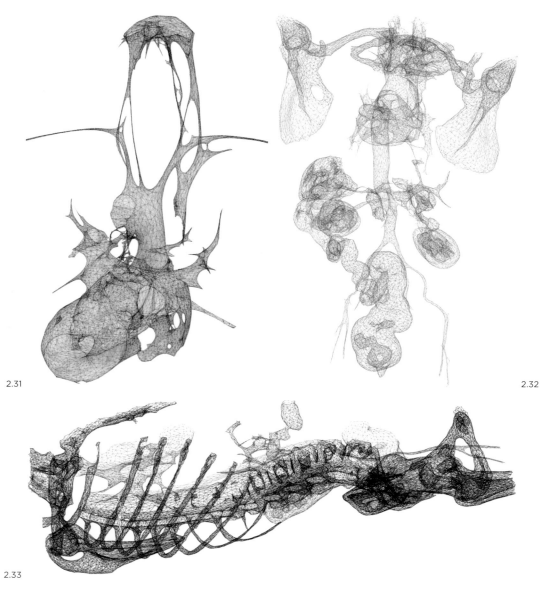

2.31

2.32

2.33

2.34

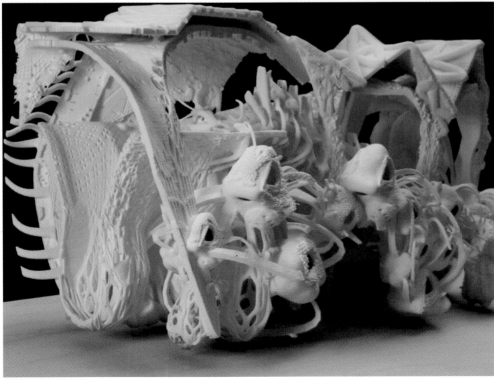

2.35

RC2 — aRC(2)himera

RC2 — aRC(2)himera

RC2 — Final Crits

RC2 — aRC(2)himera

RC2 External Examination (left to right: Guan Lee, Marjan Colletti, Evan Douglis, Tea Lim)

MArch
GAD

RESEARCH
CLUSTER

3

ALL THE WORLD'S A STAGE
Stephen Gage, Ruairi Glynn and Ollie Palmer

RC3 looks at the way that architectural objects and spaces transform over time, and at ways of designing and choreographing these transformations so that they are delightful and possibly useful to the people that observe and inhabit them. We explore the way that people perceive and take part in these transformations and also at the significance of the site, the more fixed stage in which these transformations take place, and how the site itself affects the people and objects within it.

During the past year, RC3 students discussed the nature and limits of materials in dynamic movement. Together, we looked at how objects and structures can be moved from site to site and how control systems can be programmed to move objects in different ways to give different kinds of behaviours — including automatic behaviour, responsive behaviour and fully interactive behaviour. Students built 1:1 experimental installations, but in order to do this, they had to represent what they were going to do before they made it, both to themselves and to others. This meant that different kinds of time-based representation techniques were taught, including 2D notation, 3D animation, algorithmic representation and computer coding. Students worked individually in Term 1 and in groups of three for the rest of the year. Below we have summarised some of our projects and other activities such as workshops and field trips.

Materials and objects are not neutral / Objects can perform In the first stage of this project we asked students to buy three small different objects that they liked for less than £10 in total and define not more than three desirable attributes of each object and then draw, or otherwise represent each object so that each desirable characteristic is isolated. We did this in order to find out whether our students liked minimal things, complex things, soft things, hard things, monochrome things, coloured things, patterned things, anthropomorphic things, tall thin things, short fat things, amorphous things, things with defined geometries, etc. People bring attributes to new objects. These attributes are part of people (specifically their memory) as much as they are part of the objects that they like. Object memory does not use words. It is visual, aural and haptic. We then asked students to imagine how their selected objects might put on a performance inside a 400mm x 400mm x 400mm cube. Students drew the imaginary cube in plan and section to show where the objects where placed in reference to the audience. The performance was then drawn and/or otherwise notated. Individual stop-frame animations of the object performance were filmed from two points of view — the audience's, and the designer's, who sees both the performance and the audience.

A 1:1 Installation Individual students were then asked to consider how they might construct an installation that could fit into a notional 4000mm x 4000mm x 4000mm cube. The brief was to make something that will amaze and delight the people who come to see it. It could tell a story (but not in words) or make a point. We asked the students to consider the materials from which the installation was to be built: what activates it, what it senses, its operating algorithm, its goals and responses. We asked that the final installations were represented as models at 1:10 and use it for stop frame animation, to include maquettes of the people who are the audience. Students then brought their ideas together in groups and full size experimental installations were constructed. These are illustrated on the following pages.

Specialist seminars and workshops Specialist skills and insights are required to take time-based physical installations into the 'real' world. The following seminars and workshops were offered to RC3 students in addition to those offered generally in the GAD programme:

'Automating Environments', an intensive one-week workshop in rapid prototyping of electronic and kinetic systems, joined in tandem with the Bartlett's AAC course. Run by Ruairi Glynn, Ollie Palmer and John Nussey, with Chiachi Yeh, Ciriaco Castro Diez and Huajing Liu.

'Constructing Actors', a workshop focusing on the ability to 'breathe life' into inanimate objects through the art of puppetry. Run by Ruairi Glynn and master puppeteers Pete Gunson and Eleanor Hooper.

RC3 Students: Hussnein Amin, Valentina Berardi, Cherry (Liru) Chen, Maria Hadjivasili, Ji Hye Alex Kim, Ami Kito, Nicola Kovacevic, Qi Liao, Norraniti Prougestaporn, Liang Liang Song, Xiaomeng Su, Young Jin Sunwoo, Sicong Wang, Rengran Zhang, Xun Zoe Zhou

3.1

Fig. 3.1 — 3.5 Hussnein Amin, Nicola Kovacevic and Rengran Zhang, Arm. The group commenced working by using a simple robot arm as a tool with which to understand the relationship between gesture, spatial relationship and sound. Rengran began to look at the role of gesture in authoritarian societies and developed an interest in automata and the notion of surveillance, especially in the context of recent interpretations of Jeremy Bentham's work. Nicola continued with his interest in sound, working with MaxMSP to develop a way of directly driving the arm with his saxophone and Hussnein developed an understanding of programming and control. This included working with vision systems that identified observer position and behaviour. A lot of effort went into the software "glue" that was needed to link vision software, sound software and actuation software. The group then went on to look at more complex and softer arm technologies, exploring multiple articulation and soft plywood spring mechanisms. The arm that is finally developed has multiple personalities, from a direct interactive behaviour that mimics observers and then structures further responses to give authoritarian gesture and surveillance and emotional behaviour linked to sound.

3.2

3.4

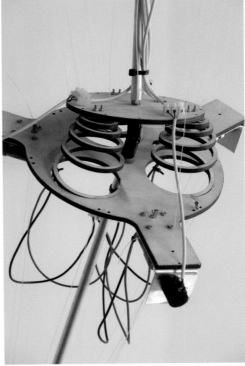

3.3

3.5

Fig. 3.6 — 3.7 Xiaomeng Su. Xiaomeng developed a concept of using modified natural forms to give light as an enrichment of urban parklands. This led her to look at way finding systems and on to the idea of human generated pheromone trails. **Fig. 3.8 — 3.9** Alex Kim. Alex worked with RC4 during term 1 constructing interactive mechanisms that were Arduino controlled. These were elegantly constructed and spatially defined. Initial conversations with Valentina and Xiaomeng led her to take a key role in accurately spatialising the group project. **Fig. 3.10** Valentina Berardi. Valentina developed an interest in pendulum mechanisms and how these can generate hypnotic objects and spaces. This led her to look at different types of chaos pendulum. She then began to speculate about ways of making a large 3 dimensional chaos pendulum and how this might be placed in a space.

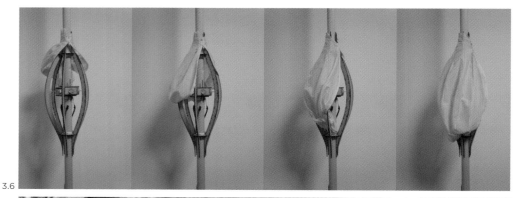

3.6

3.7

3.8

3.9

Fig. 3.11 — 3.12 Xiaomeng Su, Valentina Berardi and Alex Kim, Chaos Lab. The group project links the ideas of a 3 dimensional chaos system with a pheromone trail. Real time CFD is used to plot notional "heat plumes" generated by occupants to give a continually changing chaotic space. The CFD is projected into an array of platted translucent lines that pick up the 2D image and place it in 3 dimensions. The lines also carry cabling to LED down lights that begin to indicate a pheromone trail on the sensing floor. The work requires highly accurate projection and extensive high end CFD programming that is then linked to sensing and actuation software. Angelos Chronis acted as consultant to the group in the preparation of the CFD programme.

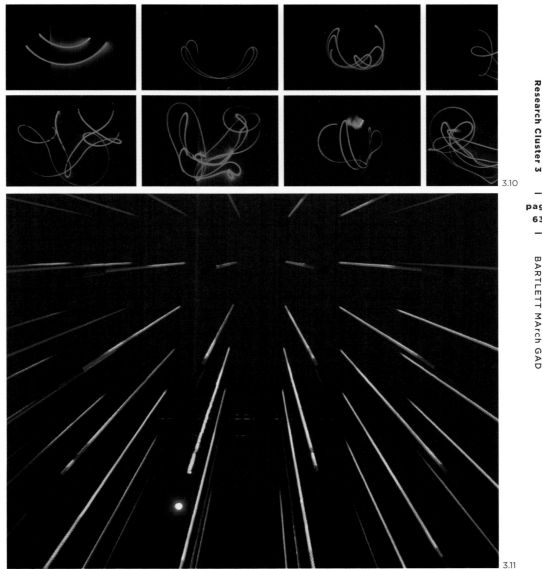

3.10

3.11

Fig. 3.13 Young Yin Sunwoo. Young Yin explored the idea of an oversized puppet that, through its behaviour, would begin to describe the self-image of its observer. Lightweight prototypes were animated in three-dimensional space, which in its turn was studied as a monumental proposition. **Fig. 3.14** Norraniti Prougestaporn. The term was spent looking at objects that floated in space. Norraniti then became interested in self image and designed projection systems based on facial recognition software with arrays of smiling and frowning balloons as an end result. **Fig. 3.15** Ami Kito. Ami explored concepts of performance in a lyrical and graphic form. The ideas extended to the notion that part of the magic of a performance in architectural as opposed to theatrical space can exist at the ceiling level rather than in direct view. She explored the idea of a world of choreographed "birds" co-existing with performance and audience and then took this idea forward to a performance by "birds" on their own.

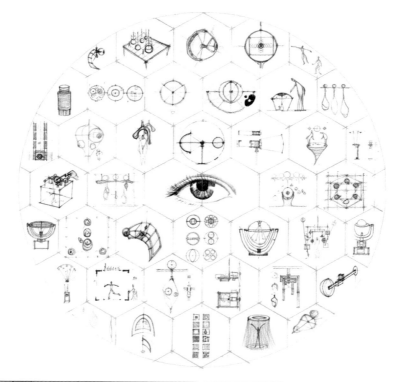

3.13

3.14

3.15

Fig. 3.12, 3.16 — 3.18 Ami Kito, Norraniti Prougestaporn and Young Jin Sunwoo, Self-Reference. The group worked on ways of merging some very strong initial concepts. They were very influenced by the ideas behind the installation by the famous cybernetician, Gordon Pask in the Cybernetics Serendipity exhibition at the ICA in 1968. In it there are three classes of protagonist: "male" robots, "female" robots and the public audience. In the group project developed four classes of protagonist are proposed: a central object that allowed an individual member of the audience to reflect on her/his own identity, an counterpoint set of "birds" that reflect the behaviour of the individual member of the audience and the central object and an audience. The project was explored through a range of media and technologies with numerous prototypes that started with a full size virtual installation. The design of the central object became an "eye" that both reflected on it's own experience and that of the observer. This involved software that sensed observer position, and drove a sphere in two axis, image capture and image projection in a confined space. Three different versions of the "birds" were produced with the final version as a form of "cambird".

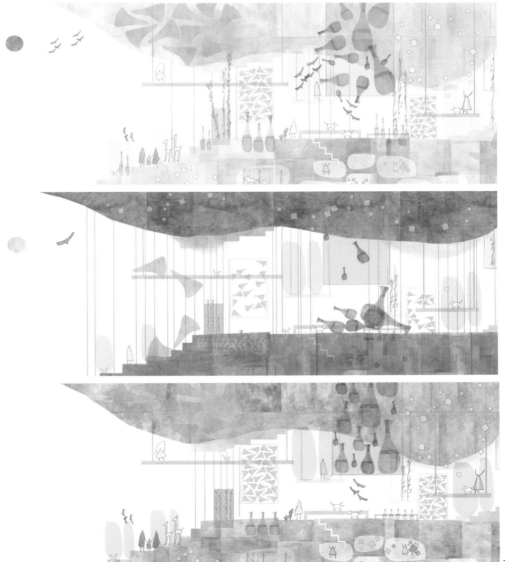

3.17

3.18

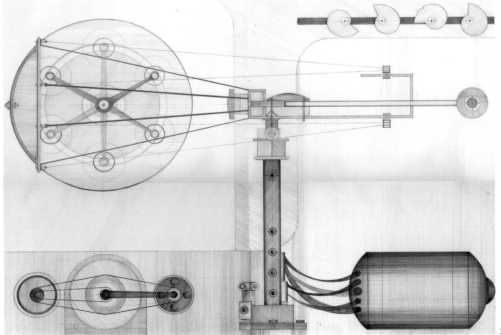

3.19

Fig. 3.20 Qi Liao. Qi has an enviable flair for producing inventive machinery that works. She proposed a space that was inhabited by a pair of huge mechanical hands in intimate conversation, and built a model that convincingly demonstrated how this might work.
Fig. 3.21 — 3.26 Liru Chen, Qi Liao and Liang Liang Song, 'Shadow Play'. Previously Liru produced shadow manipulators using drivable surfaces. These well made pieces set off an interest in the construction of shadow and its role in the making of space. The group decided to develop a shadow illusion performance that works in depth loosely based on Plato's Allegory of the Cave as a model of human perception. A set of tetrahedra of differing sizes are driven on 3 axes to interact with members of the audience who relate with them (observers in the system) while a further audience (observers of the system) view the resultant projection on a screen. The tetrahedra are manipulated by puppeteers wearing gloves with imbedded bend sensors linked to transmitters that are picked up by the actuation system. The puppeteers improvise from set pre defined responses to observer behaviour. They can either be regarded as a further class of "observer in the system" or as a precursor of a computerised version of the same. All components have been taken through multiple iterations and a special stage was built to house the performance.

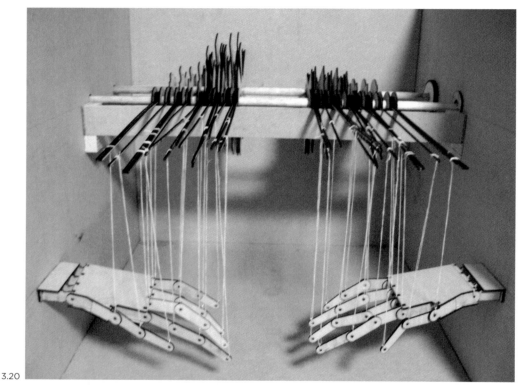

3.20

3.21

3.22

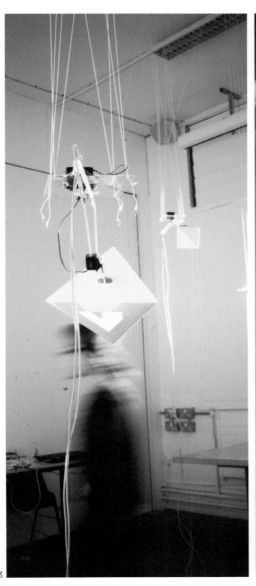

3.23

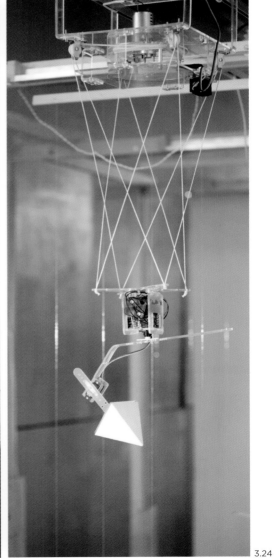

3.24

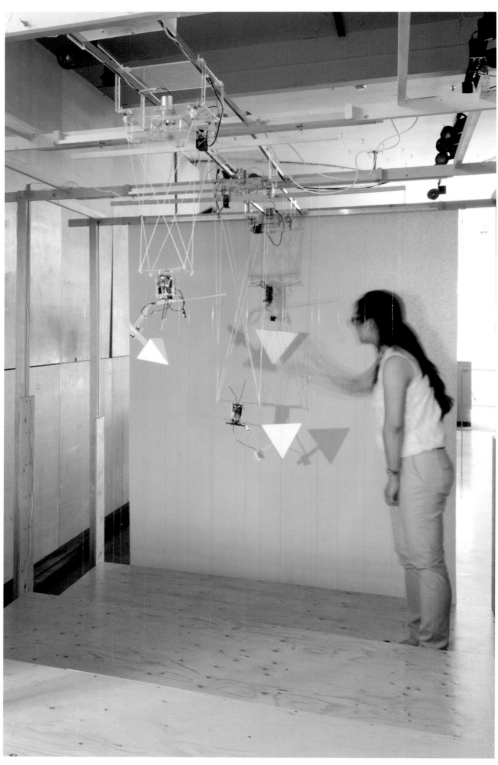

3.25

3.26

Fig. 3.27 — 3.28 Xun Zhou. Xun developed an interest in how rubber mesh installations might deform in response to presence, making delicate physical models and an interactive virtual 1:1 model using grasshopper. **Fig. 3.29** Maria Hadjivasili. Maria made spaces that as a progression through shadows, consistently experimenting with models and producing elegant photographs as a result. As the term progressed she became increasing aware of the importance light type and position. **Fig. 3.30 — 3.32** Maria Hadjivasili, Sicong Wang and Xun Zhou, 'Wall'. The group worked on an interactive shadow wall, first as a virtual installation and finally as a 1:1 physical installation. Following Xun's work in the first term the group experimented with silicone gel based soft robots that were pneumatically driven before taking the same principle to drive a skin ply and tube surface. Sicong had experience from Term 1 on 2D and 3D vision systems and how to identify the location of people and facial expression. How to use this information to drive virtual and physical installations fed into the group project. The wall is thick, with an interior and 2 exterior surfaces. It evolves its behaviour through a genetic algorithm that is varies according to the number of people that are present. Multiple, changing shadows are created in depth.

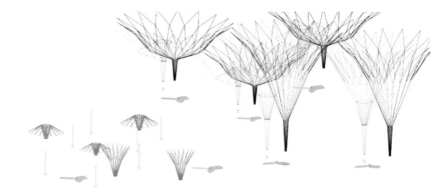

3.27

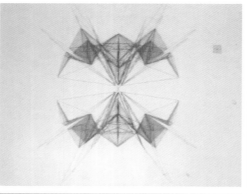

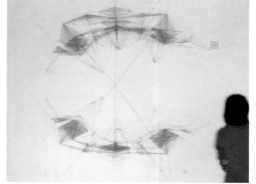

3.28

3.29

3.30

3.31

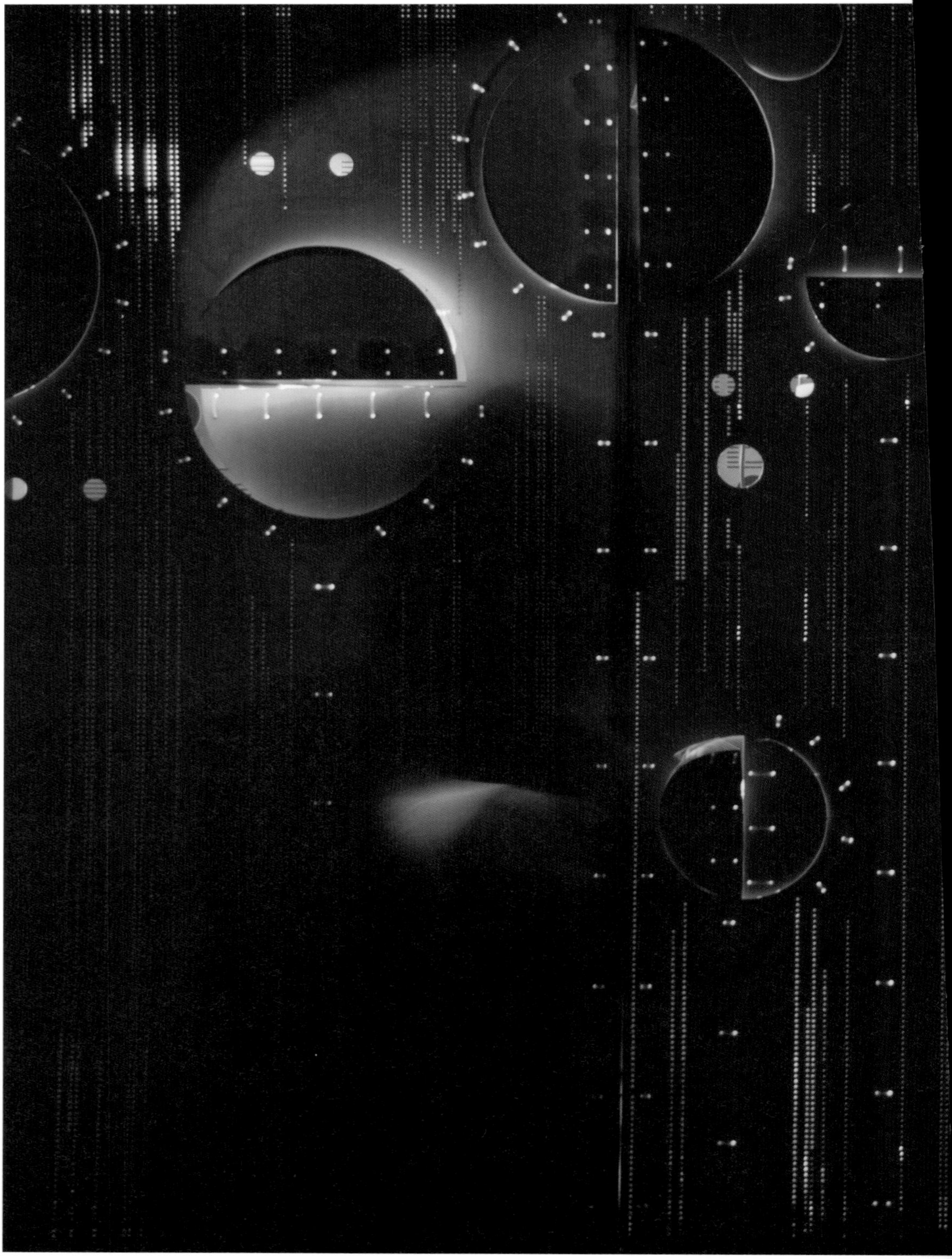

3.32

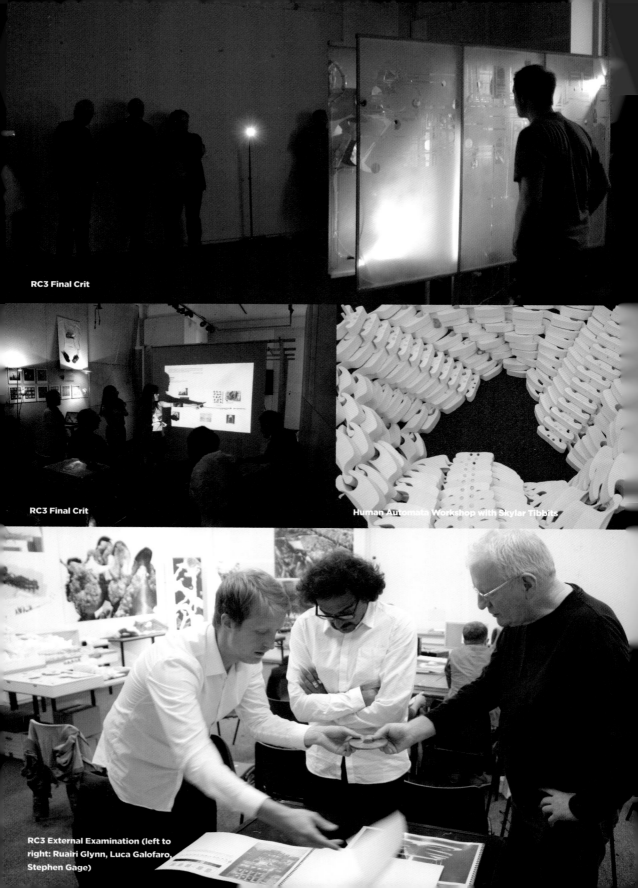

RC3 Final Crit

RC3 Final Crit

Human Automata Workshop with Skylar Tibbits

RC3 External Examination (left to right: Ruairi Glynn, Luca Galofaro, Stephen Gage)

RC3 Final Crit (left to right: Ruairi Glynn, Professor Frédéric Migayrou, Andrew Porter, Stephen Gage, Ollie Palmer, Matt Wade)

RC3 Final Crit

MArch
GAD

RESEARCH
CLUSTER

4

DIGITAL PROTOTYPING

Xavier De Kestelier, Jethro Hon

Computational design and digital fabrication are central to the research agenda of RC4. Both can be seen as architectural methodologies; the first is often perceived as a pure design methodology while the latter implies a particular method of making. Both methods can often operate individually, but we would argue that this limits its true potential. It is by hybridizing computational design and digital fabrication that we can break free of previous connotations of the digital and allow us to fully exploit the computational design potential. We are interested in a bottom-up approach where both computational design and digital fabrication is both the driver and the driven. Where both ends are interested in the digital and material processes to achieve fitness. The designer therefore becomes a listener to the behaviours in this process, and acts as one of many forces in the evolution of its design evolution.

Within architecture, the use of digital design technology has focused for years on computers as digital drafting tools. It is only in the last few years that architects have started to use computational tools as design generators / direct outputs. Computational design delivers the potential to handle large and complex sets of data, in real-time from remote locations that would otherwise be impossible to coordinate and manipulate manually or in an iterative manner. This allows us to quantify large sets of parameters from spatial to engineering aspects of design through virtual simulations. It is during simulation that we are able to evolve material and fabricational systems to subject to conditions beyond what can be find in the natural situations. These systems can be diverse but extremely precise by continuously being optimised through its response to its host environment. Optimisation as a terminology is often seen as a part of an engineering discourse, but this terminology has, through computation, found its way into the architectural design discourse.

Architectural design can often be optimised for a wide range of aspects: stiffness, strength, acoustics, assembly, material use, environmental footprint, weight, cost, etc. All of these aspects will have an impact onto the design. It is the task of the designer to decide the importance and weighing of each of these factors. More often a compromise will have to be made. The lightest structure might not be feasible from an assembly point of view or the most efficient acoustical solution might not be feasible from a cost perspective.

For RC4 we did not compromise and we concentrated on one aspect only. All thesis and design was focussed on exploring and exploiting one design aspect to the extreme. By doing this, other aspects were subdued and became of lesser importance.

We believe that true innovation can only be achieved by concentrating all effort on one aspect. This aspect will have to be researched to its limits. For example

if designing a light structure, it should almost float in thin air; if focusing
on assembly, it should become the most intelligent assembly system possible; and
if designing a collapsible structure, it should be portable on a plane.

RC4 started with three short assignments: Subtractive, Additive and Formative.
Each of these assignments introduced students to a different subclass of
fabrication techniques and digital tools. They were intertwined with short
seminars and lectures that had a tangential relationship with the particular
topic. For the first assignment teams were organized into groups of two or
three, using standard recycled material and Makedo connection pieces to develop
a response to such technology.

In Terms Two and Three, we used both digital and physical models to optimise
this one particular aspect. These digital and physical models were developed
in parallel. The physical models or processes, being for example material,
kinetic or acoustic, were verified through digital simulations and these digital
simulations and analysis were then tested through physical models. The research
towards the optimisation of design aspects was explored through both digital
and physical media.

This brief does not imply a specific site or architectural programme, but this
does not mean that the brief is not specific. On the contrary, it implies hyper
specificity towards achieving optimal intention.

Special Thanks : EOS, NetFabb GmbH, SmartGeometry, Foster + Partners, Decker
Yeadon, SOM, Richard Meiers + Partners.

RC4 Students: Paveena Amornkul, Monthira Chatinthu, Long Cheng,
Tian Chen Dai, Chuojun He, Ivan Linares Quero, Rohini Nair,
Chu-Hao Pan, Isidora Radenkovic, Javier Sandoval Bautista, Arjun Uppal

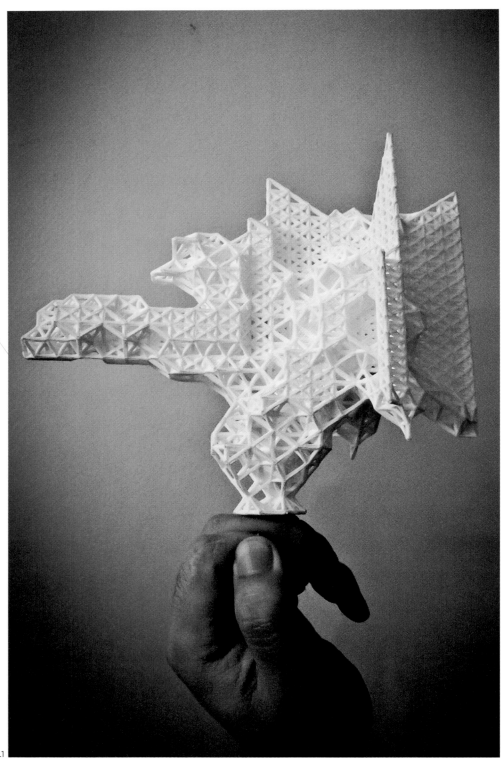

Chu-Hao Pan, Using Cellular Automata for an adaptive and dynamic architecture. This project contains two parts. The first part is to research Cellular Automata and develop a robust system with the Cellular Automata (CA) rules tested and developed for an adaptive and dynamic architecture. The second part integrates human interaction via a kinetic camera to grow a virtual, stable architectural structure. As a powerful tool in architectural design, CA can intelligently simulate a complex structure and optimise to fit the real world demands such as stability. In this project, the structure continuously recalculates to ensure it stabilises without any extra force and torque. The resultant of the sum of all forces ($\sum$ F) and the sum of the moment of all the forces ($\sum$ M) must be zero. **Fig. 4.1** 3D print of computer simulated structure reaching stability. **Fig. 4.2** Library of 130 possible CA growth rules. **Fig. 4.3** Iterative generations of structure stabilizing over time. **Fig. 4.4** Time generations over a digitized physical environment. **Fig. 4.5** Physical interaction with a virtual environment.

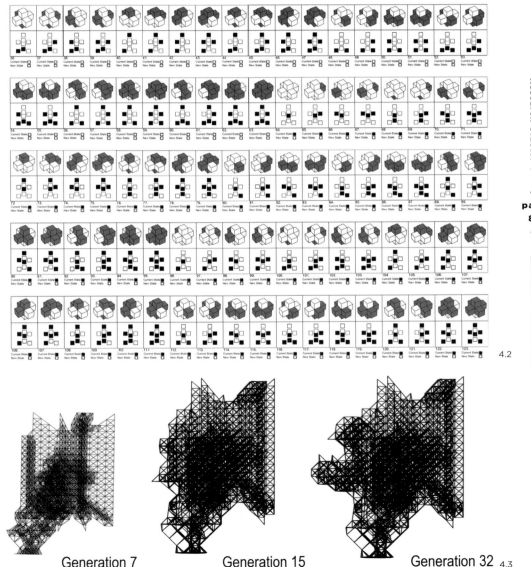

4.2

Generation 7   Generation 15   Generation 32 4.3

Scale 1:50

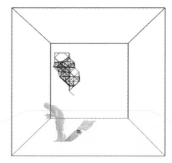

Scale 1:50

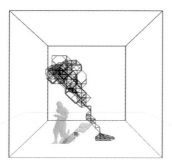

Scale 1:50

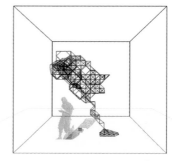

Scale 1:50

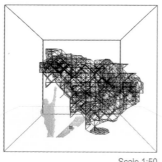

Scale 1:50

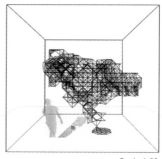

Scale 1:50

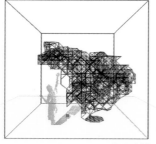

Scale 1:50

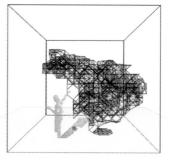

Scale 1:50

4.4

4.5

Long Cheng, '48 deg'. Structure. This work explored the relationship between simulation and fabrication through an iterative design process that alternates between physical and digital model. The work related to various form-finding techniques that investigate and simulate the interrelatedness of geometry, structure, and form. The main parametric modeling tool is the Grasshopper plug-in for the 3D modeling program Rhino. Using this generative design environment, beginning attempts try to explore how to abstract the principles learned in the physical models into digital parametric models. After digital simulation, the core endeavour is to realize the emergence effect to the real world with an optimal fabrication method. **Fig. 4.6** Detail of a tensegrity structure prototype. **Fig. 4.7** States of tensegrity structure as tension is applied. **Fig. 4.8** Photo of prototype when fully tensioned. **Fig. 4.9** Diagram of fabrication process.

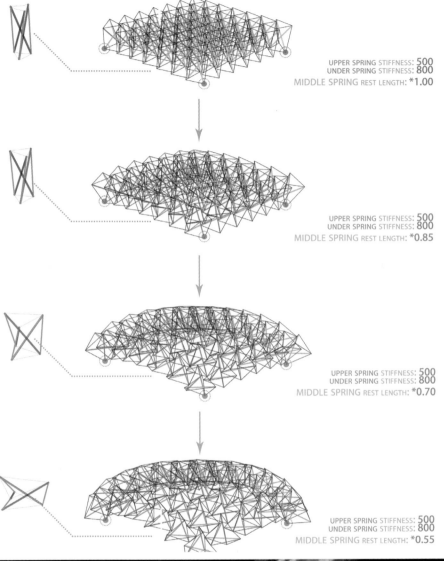

UPPER SPRING STIFFNESS: **500**
UNDER SPRING STIFFNESS: **800**
MIDDLE SPRING REST LENGTH: ***1.00**

UPPER SPRING STIFFNESS: **500**
UNDER SPRING STIFFNESS: **800**
MIDDLE SPRING REST LENGTH: ***0.85**

UPPER SPRING STIFFNESS: **500**
UNDER SPRING STIFFNESS: **800**
MIDDLE SPRING REST LENGTH: ***0.70**

UPPER SPRING STIFFNESS: **500**
UNDER SPRING STIFFNESS: **800**
MIDDLE SPRING REST LENGTH: ***0.55**

4.7

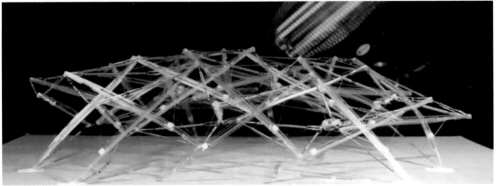

4.8

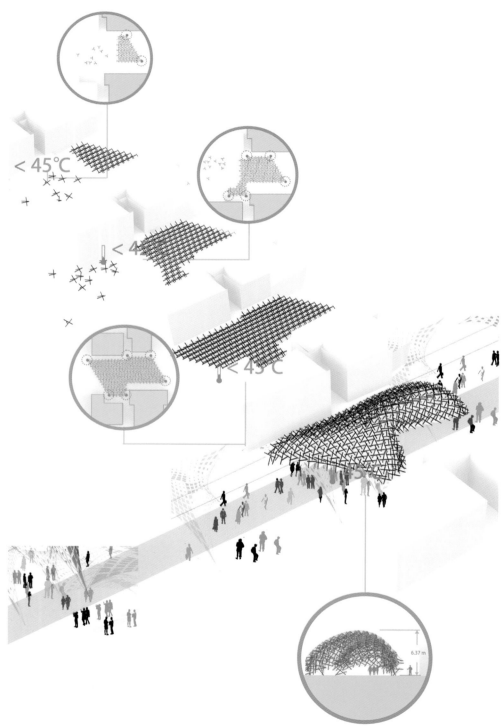

< 45°C

< 4

< 45°C

6.37 m

Monthira Chatinthu, 'Performative Morphology'. This project aimed to design a bamboo structure by researching performative morphology and material performance. It was inspired by a study on the weaving of a spider web, which is also used for catching prey. The interest here was in investigating how to design and construct a new woven structure by utilizing the capability and performance of materials. One of the outstanding points extracted from the study on spider webs was the weaving technique which is similar to the spider creating the structure of its web. To design the bamboo structure, an analysis was also conducted to integrate mathematical principles in terms of geodesic patterns. There are several advantages of bamboo such as rapid growth, high flexibility, and good resistance to hot and cold weather. **Fig. 4.10** Physical prototype of bamboo woven pillar. **Fig. 4.11** Rendering showing the pillar weaving into a canopy.

4.10

4.11

Isidora Radenkovic and Paveena Amornkul, 'Fog Harvesting'. Resources strains, particularly water, diminish the quality of life of billions of people. This research proposes a potentially new source of fresh water that relies on the process of fog harvesting, inspired by the microstructure of the Namibian fog-harvesting beetle. Using 3D printing technology and a fog chamber, constructed to simulate the Namib Desert environment, provided a reliable testing facility for experimentation. This enabled us to determine the most efficient prototype under appropriate conditions. Moreover, Netfabb software allowed us to transform the micro-prototypes into a complex architectural structure. By shifting the density of the micro cells, this created the performance differentiation between fog harvesting and support cells. A hexagonal skeleton where each side of the hexagon is used as a base for the fog harvesting panels. Condensed water is channeled by the geometry of the structure, and directed down panels via hanging water delivery units, called, stalactites. This project provides nomadic Topnaar tribe with shelter from and provide a source of fresh water that is easily accessible and transportable. **Fig. 4.12** SLS print of a scaled structure to harvest water. **Fig. 4.13** Data measuring performances of various micro-structures. **Fig. 4.14** Fog chamber and physical testing of dew collection. **Fig. 4.15** Rendering of gradient cell geometries. **Fig. 4.16** Rendering of the 3D printed structure situated in the Namib desert. **Fig. 4.17** Rendering illustrating potential end-user inhabitation.

4.12

CELL TYPE:
ring

CELL SIZE:
6mm

36 ml

Quantity of water collected after conducting the fog simulation for 20 minutes in the chamber

The ring prototype gave the best results on both digital and physical simulations. The design feature of the ring allows the contraction and expantion of the fabricated prototypes. The diversity of features as well as the best condensation rate stipulate the continuing the project development with this design.

Large scale micro cell prototype

Pre Filter Measurements

Post Filter Measurements

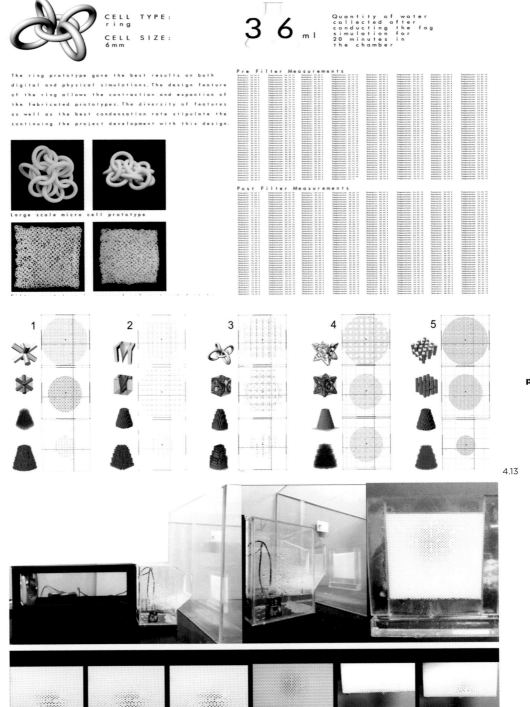

1 2 3 4 5

4.13

4.14

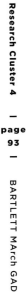

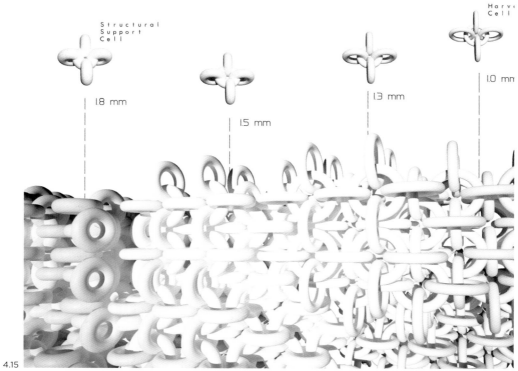

Structural
Support
Cell

Harve
Cell

1.8 mm

1.5 mm

1.3 mm

1.0 mm

4.15

4.16

4.17

Ivan Linares Quero, 'Clouds'. Following the works of Frei Otto Air-structures, the research project called Clouds Manifesto, has been exploring the limits of lighter-than-air structures. The two main goals proposed during the last months were, first, the creation of a whole independent family of possible structures and applications to the environment, from multiple scales, configuration, functions and systems. Secondly, the construction of a physical prototype able to float for long time by itself. This prototype, called AirBrick, is a cube (due reasons of assemblage and flooring) ready to float using a new low energy consuming system based on self-density regulation. Several airbags are connected to ultra-light micro-pumps controlled by different sensors. Information from sensors is processed in the micro-controller brain in order to pump in and suck out air from the environment to the airbags. **Fig. 4.18** Physical prototype of a floating 'AirBrick'. **Fig. 4.19** Carbon frame, helium balloon, airbags, electronics within the prototype cube. **Fig. 4.20** Urban scenario 1. **Fig. 4.21** Urban scenario 2.

4.18

4.19

4.20

4.21

Tian-Chen Dai and Chuo-Jun He, 'Smart Module, Hyper Metabolism'. The project 'Smart Module, Hyper Metabolism' is based base on research of local to global modular system. This is a project optimises the density of a group of components through local to global transformation. Combining the thoughts of self-assembly and local to global thoughts, the project has been developed to have a self-intelligence in connecting and be able to optimize the density of the system through transformation of single unit. In the end, the density of the shadow has been chosen as the element the system aims to optimize. Through a series of material and moving studies, the design has been achieved through magnet connections and NiTi spring. **Fig. 4.22** Installation of Smart Modules.

Fig. 4.23 Modules magnetic 3D printed connection design. **Fig. 4.24** Shadow studies of the prototype modules contracting.

4.22

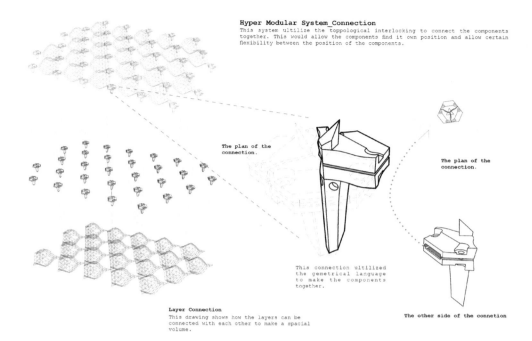

Hyper Modular System_Connection

This system ultilize the toppological interlocking to connect the components together. This would allow the components find it own position and allow certain flexibility between the position of the components.

The plan of the connection.

The plan of the connection.

This connection ultilized the gemetrical language to make the components together.

The other side of the connetion

Layer Connection

This drawing shows how the layers can be connected with each other to make a spacial volume.

4.23

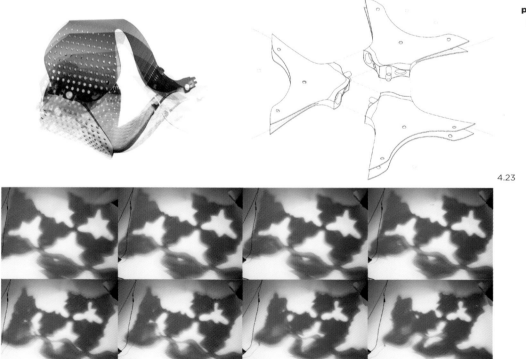

4.24

Rohini Nair, 'Wind Breaker'. The objective of this research project is to create a passive screen or instalment that is able to divert the high speed winds and reduce its speed as it pass through this screen. Wind is a powerful natural force, blocking it completely is not always a good option as this ends up increasing the lateral force on the screen. Therefore diverting it, along with reduction of speed, helps reduce the wind load on it. The aim is to create a geometry that would do this passively. To achieve this, various fabric stitched geometries, inspired by nature, were tested and bunched together in a specific pattern. Placed at strategic locations on a tall building they reduce the wind load. **Fig. 4.25** Rendering of wind breaker creating texture over a building facade. **Fig. 4.26** Time lapse photo of the prototype.

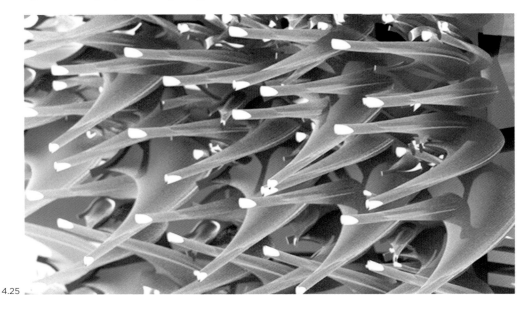

4.25

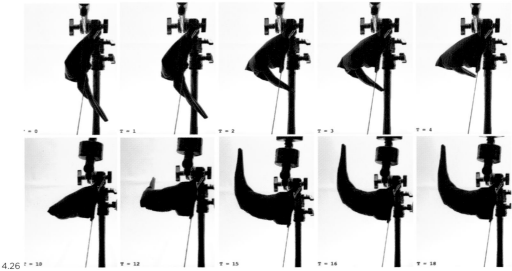

4.26

Arjun Uppal, 'Morphological Dynamism in Architecture'. This project aims to achieve a direct dynamic response to rainfall as a stimulus by studying the movement of the motor cells in the pulvinus of the Mimosa Pudica plant. The system within the project uses desiccant material and its properties when subject to rainfall or moisture are used to drive the system. The distribution of desiccants on the surface of the umbrella gradually give the system structural strength. The entire system works in direct response to rainfall and slowly closes or comes back to its original state when rainfall stops. **Fig. 4.27** Silica gel before and after absorption of moisture. **Fig. 4.28** Network of silica gels stimulating movement of a canopy. **Fig. 4.29** Rendering of the skeleton network over the structure.

Javier Sandoval Batista, 'Apertures/Porosity in Envelopes'. The Gill Project is a modular façade system inspired by the performance and shape of the gill, using SMA (Shape Memory Alloy Materials) such as Nitinol Springs to create a system of apertures, without any computational or electrical device, just an understanding of the performance of the material. Acting like a living and breathing skin, it allows a building to express, communicate and interact and response with its environment. **Fig. 4.30** Heat sensitive springs detail triggering facade opening. **Fig. 4.31** Mechanism retracting the wood veneer. **Fig. 4.32** Physical working prototype of the facade system.

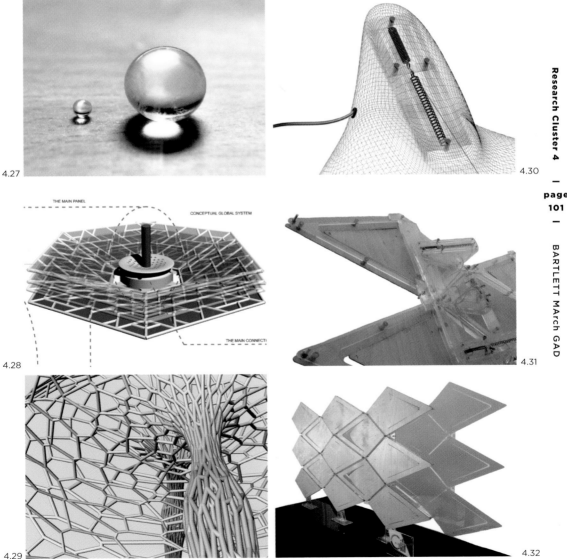

4.27

4.30

4.28

4.31

4.29

4.32

RC4 Final Presentation (left to right: Bruce Davidson, Xavier de Kestelier, Hugh Whitehead, Jethro Hon)

RC4 Workshop

RC4 Field Trip to New York City

RC4 MArch GAD students participating in the 2012 Smart Geometry event at the Rensselaer Polytechnic Institute, Troy, USA

RC4 setting up a 3D printer

RC4 Workshop

RC4 Final Crits (left to right: Andrew Porter, Professor Stephen Gage, Xavier de Kestelier, Hugh Whitehead)

MArch GAD

RESEARCH CLUSTER

5

[RE]CALIBRATOR

Andrew Porter, Luke Pearson

Architects in the modern world find themselves in a quandary. For so long the clearly defined path between sketch, drawing and structure could be seen as a sliding scale. How do we deal with our thought process as architects in a world where the illusion of this progression may well have been shattered? What is the position of the sketch in a digital age where rather than going through a process of refinement, the lines and movements may be translated directly into architectural fabric themselves? Is this a process of concurrent translation, the act of flowing notations and interpretations being constantly fed back and forth — as if it were between multi-lingual aides shaping policies through networks of differing dialects at the United Nations?

Architecture has many established frameworks, dialects of drawing that we understand to be reference points for communicating architectures through — representation. These have, in most cases, existed for many years. Yet the very idea of a sequential process of architectural resolution hanging from these frameworks is being constantly challenged by new innovations and techniques — in software.

We investigated novel, hybridised approaches towards the architectural drawing that constituted engagement with appropriated codifications (programming, processing, computation) to take advantage of the potentiality of an interplay between the haptic, the intuitive, and the rational.

The haptic suggests direct manipulation of a material upon a substrate in order to generate a result — the cluster researched new definitions of this condition in a world that may be composed of digital materials and simulated substrates. Are there clues in the way machine outputs translate our movements into choreographies of milling, gluing and solidifying that may give us new tactics for approaching drawing and indeed questioning the materiality of the outputs of these processes. The ubiquity of the off-white 3d print as digital sketch belies the fact that we already have a wide gamut of tools and materials to express our architectural intentions. How can we question this material itself and how we may manipulate it, to emphasis the inherent difference between a digital drawing and a rapid prototype?

The potential clarity of translation between gesture — software — hardware has an immediacy that returns architecture to a (new) sense of craft. On he other hand, the potential lack of clarity within these translations, or the missteps and misshapes that occur — can instigate new edge conditions between the haptic and the manufactured. By approaching the idea of architectural representation as an act of assemblage, the cluster proposed reconciliation and investigation into the materialities produced by new manufacturing technologies as part of hybridised architectures that existed as mediators between these translatory territories. As the process of digital translation slides back and forth, it will apply progressive distortions onto our idea of what it is to delineate space. Through the development of new conventions of drawing to be able to quantify this feedback — the architect can reclaim aspects of their field new technology allows them to expropriate and then manifest ways of drawing these new conditions.

A sizeable proportion of architects remain haptic creatures. Many practices who appear as key proponents of the "digital" agenda are led by those using "traditional" tools and thought structures to first derive designs. Our cluster did not propose to merely remove the gestural in favour of codifications and generators, but to understand how the notion of the gesture in architectural — production has been altered by its interpolation through computation.

RC5 wishes to design these processes of translation, and the new drawn — methodologies that emerge through their computational interpolation. Through investigation into the interplay of physical and digital assemblage the cluster developed a new position vis-à-vis contemporary architectural representation, and the direction in which new technologies of manufacture may or may not shift it. We believe that the epistemological ground upon which architecture sits is shifting, but that working into the gaps and niches that emerge in the fabric of our understanding will allow us to derive an architecture that calibrates itself through a careful balancing act.

By jacking open these fissures, RC5 students conjured fluctuating architectural zones. Zones where waste plastic particulates in the sea become subsumed into nano-assembled fractal monoliths, or calligraphic architectures terraforming an island in the memory of a great Korean master. Zones defining a new conception of 'air space' and its political capital through pressure thresholds or a furtive architecture that evades scanning technologies. Other territories were painted onto the city directly with light to capture fleeting apparitions or planted a glitch into our everyday navigation systems. These architectures became the manifestation of translatory tensions, calibratory frameworks for traversing new architectural borderlands.

RC5 Students: Rebecca Fox, Michail Karolos Keranis, Margarita Koulilourdi, Yunan Lin, Phillip Mandery, Lilit Mnatsakanyan, Maj Plemenitas, Ian Bernard Slover, Anthoula Tzakou, Ping Ping Xia, Nikki (Yuxin) Xie, Hyejin Yang, Huading Zhang

Fig. 5.1 — 5.4 Maj Plemenitaš, 'LINK 10⁻⁹][10⁹'. Can something that is striving for stability also act as a perceptive and receptive medium for active and passive exchange that enables and promotes connectivity, consequently providing a vital link for a truly resilient system? **Fig. 5.1** The Node — Resilience Through Redundancy. **Fig. 5.2** In Progress_No.1192 **Fig. 5.3** From Within. **Fig. 5.4** Shifting Grounds.

/ 5.2

5.3

5.5

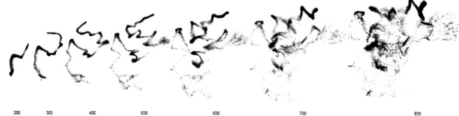

200   300   400   500   600   700   800

5.6

Fig. 5.5 Hyejin Yang, 'Calligraphy Written in Landscape'. The legacy of master Korean calligrapher Chusa is manifest through a series of digital tools developed through an analysis of the constructional movements that define the characters. By using agents and simulations of the qualities of speed, pressure, ink spread the project defines a series of tools whereby the landscape of Jeju Island in Korea can be terraformed as if by the hand of Chusa. **Fig. 5.6** Hyejin Yang, 'Calligraphy Written in Landscape'. By developing a hiking trail through a series of these landscape impositions, the project proposes a series of ephemeral architectures that emerge from momentary conglomerations of rock dust. Architectural emanations along the trail assert the legacy of Chusa as part of the rich body of artistic appropriation of landscape as part of Korean artistic culture. The development of digital tools allows for the transferral and interpolation of the gestural qualities of the calligraphic approach to start to define architecture spaces and write the legacies of the grand master onto the landscape. **Fig. 5.7** Hyejin Yang, 'Calligraphy Written in Landscape'. The gesture inspired by Chusa style calligraphy carves the bare soils of the site on Jeju Island. As this carving occurs, the landscape is also affected by the wind and surrounding environment. The ink particulates of the gesture, carve and pull the soil particles through computed collisions. As a result, a typology of calligraphic spaces are generated within the landscape.

5.7

Fig. 5.8 — 5.9 Nikki Xie, 'I Sense How You Feel'. Inspired by Cleve Backster's experiments into the 'emotions' exhibited by plants through electrical impulses, the project proposes a digital garden where this invisible landscape of data exchange constitutes a new order of sensory engagement. Through responsive hydraulic systems and a homogenised skin containing hydroponic networks, the garden reads and responds to occupation through the reaction of its plant life. **Fig. 5.10 — 5.11** Yunan Lin, 'National Museum of Computing'. The envelope of the museum is the culmination of research into the creation of a 'furtive' architecture. Through testing and understanding the potentiality of the 3D scanner, the project questions how we may subvert it through a knowledge of the interpolative process the device goes through. By discussing the potential of mirrored surface, opacities and density of laminations, the project seeks to develop a furtive architecture that shifts and responds not only to avoid resolution by mapping technologies, but also to maintain the complicated thermal requirements of a building containing arcane and power hungry computers at Bletchley Park, Buckinghamshire.

5.8

5.9

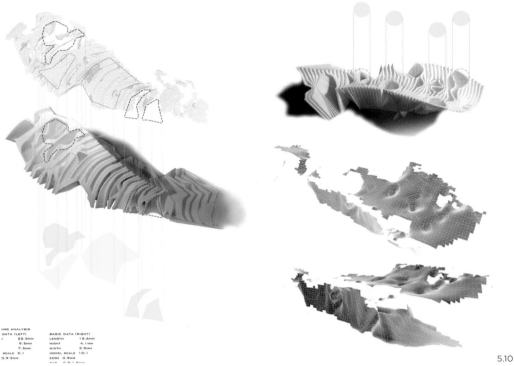

ING ANALYSIS
DATA (LEFT)
    22.5MM
    9.5MM
    7.5MM
SCALE 5:1
0.9-3MM

BASIC DATA (RIGHT)
LENGTH   12.6MM
HIGHT   4.1MM
WIDTH   3.9MM
MODEL SCALE 10:1
EDGE 0.9MM

5.10

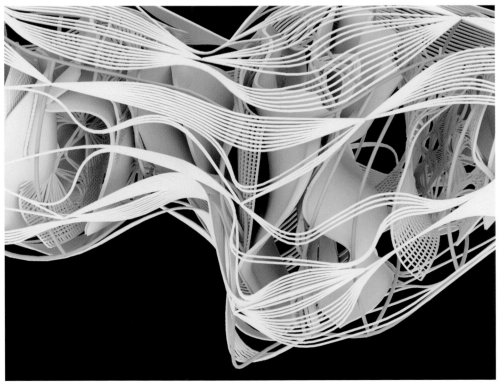

5.11

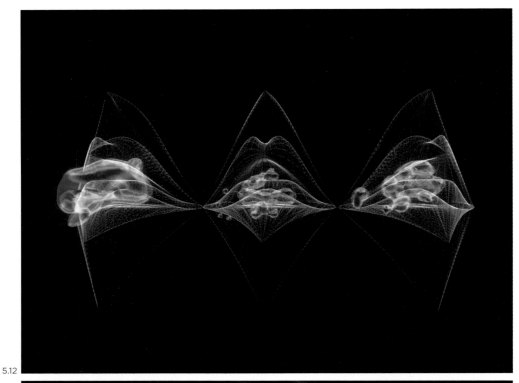

Fig. 5.12 — 5.13 Rebecca Fox, 'Furtive Terrains'. Examinations into the cosmological relationship between light and heat result in the production of a series of surfaces for trapping and propagating moss spores. The design proposes a series of articulated surfaces designed by the dispersion paths of moss spores and the ideal conditions for their maximal growth. The system can reconcile different conditions of light and shadow, dry and damp, as the individual elements adjust to atmospheric moisture, sunlight, and temperature. The project traces the cosmological impact of the sun and the solar system down to the microscopic scale of the individual spore. **Fig. 5.14** Michail Karolos Keranis, 'Designing with Light, Designing in Space'. Our perception of architectural design derives directly from our perception of space. It is also a fact that we perceive space by its interaction, and ours, with light. The project asserts light as a design material and involves the development of a syntactical body of tools. By designing with light the project aims would be able to better understand its qualities, attributes, as well as, capabilities as an instrument for creating architecture. These architectural gestures are drawn directly onto the temporal city, revealing its multifarious lives and spatial territories.

5.14

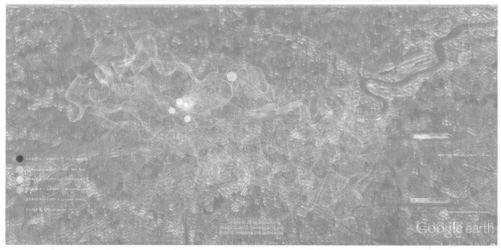

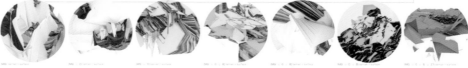

5.15

Fig. 5.15 Anthoula Tzakou, 'Software Origami'. The protocol problem of getting false data across a network is the chosen communication medium to create the simulation of a simulation of a space. This earthworks project for a decaying digital earth, visualizes a yet unsignified global representation of the 'real world' — as Google suggests — at the times when the relics of the current Internet 3.0 will be traced in future versions of the World Wide Web. Introducing another organization of perception [alongside those of space and time] involving the structure of digital data manipulated to build those virtualities. Open file types are bent to structure personalized data exchange rules and temporarily hack the software's reading algorithms and digital domains' uploading/sharing protocols. **Fig. 5.16 — 5.17** Huading

Zhang, 'The Uncertain Garden'. The multifarious histories and notorieties of St. Paul's cathedral guide the design of a landscape that articulates the preservation of the image of the building through protected sight lines. Delving into the history and constructional frameworks of anamorphosis, the project proposes an unfolding environment that unwittingly draws the inhabitant into a historical exposition of the cathedral.

5.16

5.17

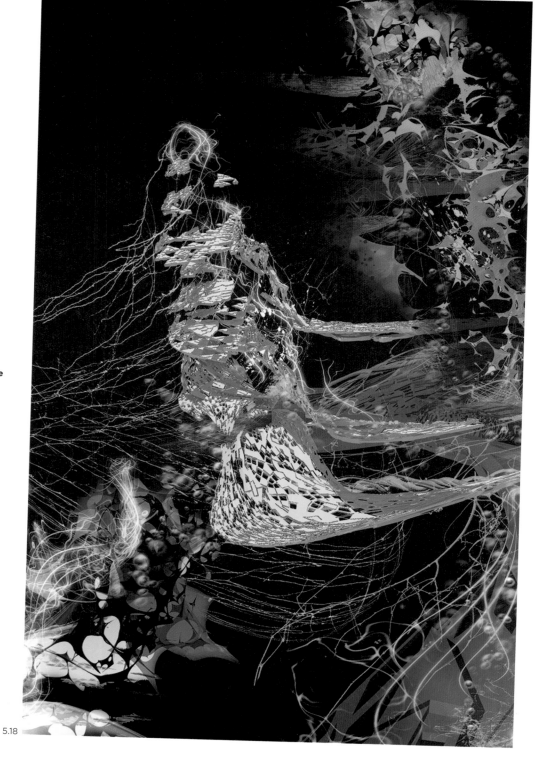

Fig. 5.18 Ping Ping Xia, 'The Layered Pier at Felixstowe'. The pier contains three different layers at the same time, its accurate and concrete existence in real world, as a whole; its future in imagination and its impression in memories, as fragments. Through its relationship to the swell of the ocean, the breeze of the wind, and the shifting of the sand, the pier becomes a pivot where the world of physical phenomena, memory and structure intertwine.

Fig. 5.19 — 5.20 Philip Mandery, 'Spatial Deanimation'. Inserting cinematic 'Fissions' into Berlin, the architecture acts as a cloud suggesting viewing corridors and the physical edge of an ephemeral boundary zone. Inspired by the Berlin of Wim Wenders, these 'durate' drawings explore an architecture that striates time and space through a series of interpolations. These fissions create a physical space that allows one to inhabit multiple zones at once through the cross hatch of filmic, historical and contemporary architectural spaces.

5.19

5.20

5.21

Fig. 5.21 Ian Bernard Slover, 'Machines for Reading and Writing Shape'. Build+grow; integration of inosculate matter into one continuous vasculature. Scaffolding trains semi-epiphytic matter into specific geometries. Use of Computer Numeric Control machines on a rigid scaffolding proliferates localized details to arrange and promote growth of substrates. To live is to produce. Growth of structural substances interspersed with assemblage of standard building methods. A structural matrix subdivides in scale to support specified program that is initially coextensive with a three dimensional symmetric coordinate system but is quickly introduced to a broad range of geometric adjacencies. **Fig. 5.22 — 5.24** Lilit Mnatasankayan, 'Through 2.5D'. The project focuses on the physical reconstruction of digital forms derived through gestural inputs. By asserting a number of feedback loops, architectural incidences emerge at points of divergence between the digital and physical. Dissecting forms and slumping materials across moulds asserts the difference between the limits and liberties of digital and physical materialities. **Fig. 5.25** Margarita Koulikourdi, 'Hidden Landscapes of Air'. The research examines the unseen zones within our surroundings. This research focuses on the huge amount of data, forces and dynamics that populate the 'perceptual void' of air, and the datascapes they create. This void space becomes an uninhabited architectural territory that striates the disputed terrain of Nicosia in Cyprus.

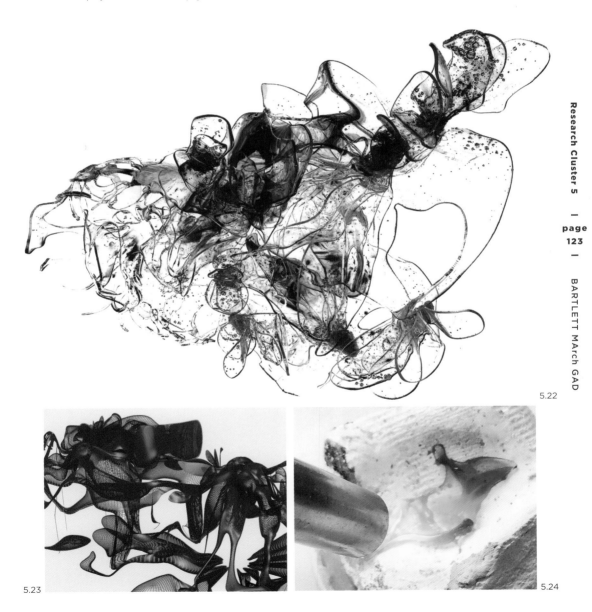

5.22

5.23

5.24

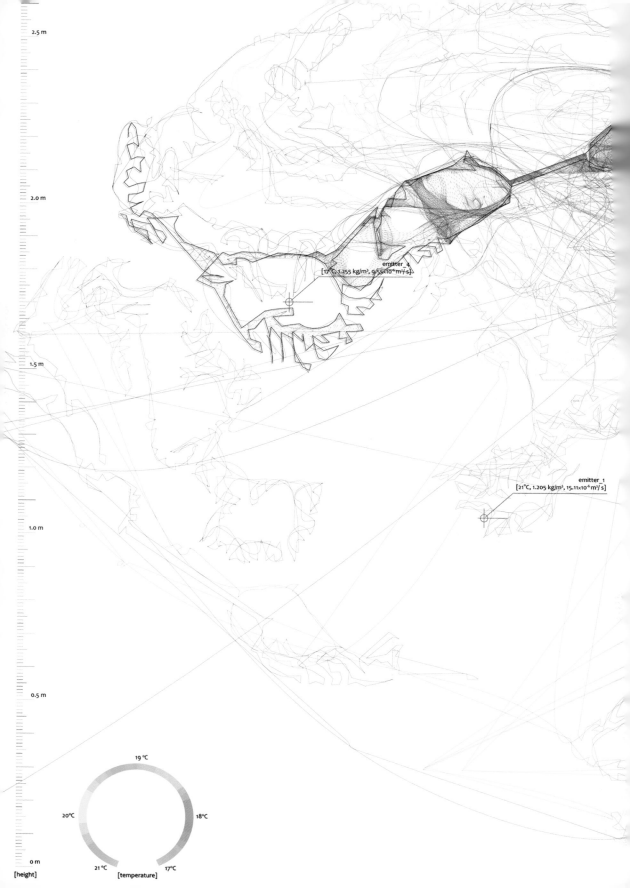

2.5 m

2.0 m

emitter_4
[17°C, 1.255 kg/m³, 9.55×10⁻⁶ m²/s]

1.5 m

emitter_1
[21°C, 1.205 kg/m³, 15.11×10⁻⁶ m²/s]

1.0 m

0.5 m

19 °C

20°C   18°C

0 m

21 °C   17°C

[height]   [temperature]

emitter _
[19°C, 1.324 kg/m³, 9.55×10⁻⁶ m²/s

emitter _2
[18°C, 1.233kg/m³, 16.97×10⁻⁶ m²/s

emitter   [temperature, density, kinematic viscosity]

mid-contour

contour line

particle distribution

mesh depiction of the air's initial volume

Human Automata Workshop with Skylar Tibbits

RCS Field Trip to Solar Power plant in southern Spain

Matias del Campo evaluating a final submission

MArch GAD

RESEARCH CLUSTER

6

MULTI-PARAMETER DYNAMICS: GENERATIVE COMPUTATIONAL DESIGN IN TIME-BASED ARCHITECTURE

Daniel Widrig, Fulvio Wirz

One of the main objectives of architecture has always been analysing natural and physical phenomena — evaluating their potential or learning from their limits — using this territory of investigation as a substrate to embed proportion, articulation and beauty within the design process. In recent research agendas, nature is no longer considered as an archetypical idea of perfection that architecture wants to metaphorically represent or imitate. Rather, it gives an opportunity to borrow highly refined processes from real life that can be used to synthesise efficient yet intricate spaces emerging from self-organised systems. Since Frei Otto's formulation in the 1950s, this approach has also been known as 'form-finding'.

Following the development of computational design in architecture the discipline now needs to redefine traditional form-finding methods, based on a single-parameter empirical study, moving towards a multi-parameter dynamic approach more suitable to represent contemporary societal complexities. This is only possible if real-world phenomena simulation interacts with project-based data, embracing the entire design cycle from concept to materialisation. In that scenario, a purely performance-driven design could arguably be considered simplistic since it relies only on one of the possible logical relations a designer can set through computation. Connecting, partitioning, layering, differentiating and scaling are some of the operations that concur in defining spatial complexity and articulation. A successful design is one able to control multiple operations, or criteria, through a lawful set of data. This system of correlations can be defined via scripting or, if it is appropriate, by using physically accurate simulation engines natively embedded in a particular software. The design process, once informed by a dynamic set of rules, can handle multiple tasks as subsets of the overall design algorithm: complex zoning strategies can emerge from intricate pathway studies, skin patterns can seamlessly correlate to the structural layout of the building. The design process evolves in a 'design-system' able to perform at multiple scales adapting to different programmes and contexts and producing several possible outcomes.

Although this level of complexity and interactivity is achievable using only the computational capabilities of individual packages, it is only through blending conceptual components and design strategies of various software that it is possible to develop and apply custom processes of form generation taking advantage of the full spectrum of possibilities offered by these systems.

RC6 explores generative computational design systems as tools to create time-based architectural space. Embracing architectural design, less as a response to market requests, but rather as a framework for spatio-social experimentation, the studio implements prototypical architectural form within existing junk space sprawling in London's urban fabric. Eventually plugging into local infrastructure these adaptive structures have the potential to re-qualify, alter or extend their immediate environment and potentially expand. Spatial complexity is tackled by developing a design system able to perform at different scales within an existing urban scenario through a unique and coherent generative process. Ideal prototype sites to test the adaptability and scalability of the design systems are neglected public spaces like facades, rooftops or gaps between buildings. Sub-systems, where used as a design strategy, must be lawfully correlated to each part of the project showing a logical placement within the overall design process.

The agenda also focuses on the development of the large-scale project with particular attention on the research of innovative material systems and manufacturing techniques also in regard to the temporary nature of the projects. This is achieved with a multidisciplinary approach, taking advantage of experts from other disciplines to define strategies, acting as a bridge between the digital model and its physical counterpart. Interim and final mock-ups and physical models of the projects play an important role by verifying the consistency of the research while getting a deeper understanding of real-world implications.

RC6 Students: Pinar Calisir, Yuxiang Cao, Yin Gao, Chao Gao, Maria Gavelli, Jin Huang, Pegah Jalaly, Fatima Khatami, Lisa Kinnerud, Gopal Sankaranarayanan, Anamaria-Beatrice Spulber, Fei Wang, Wei Wei Wei, Secil Zontur

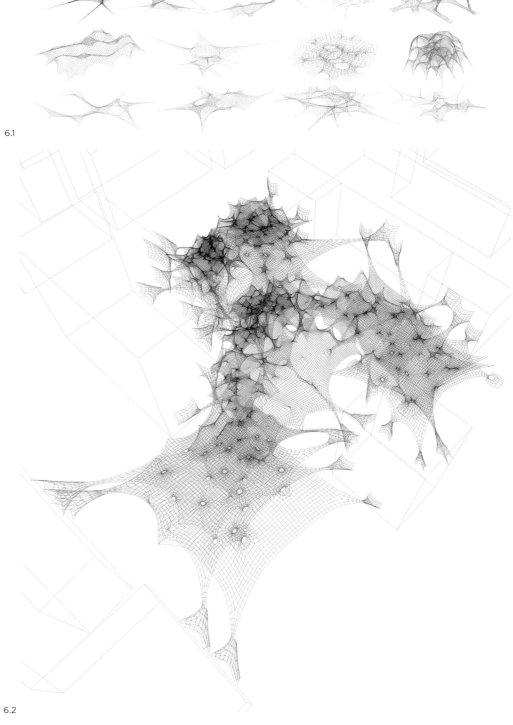

6.1

6.2

Fig. 6.1 Yin Gao, Chao Gao, Jin Huang, 'MutateBrane': Library of relaxed surfaces and initial experiments employing digital membrane simulation. **Fig. 6.2** Yin Gao, Chao Gao, Jin Huang, 'MutateBrane': Bird's eye perspective of the architectural proposal occupying a neglected public space along Tottenham Court Road. **Fig. 6.3** Yin Gao, Chao Gao, Jin Huang, MutateBrane: Northeast elevation. **Fig. 6.4** Yin Gao, Chao Gao, Jin Huang, 'MutateBrane': Structural analysis performed to optimise the overall shape and distribution of structural members in the system. The texture map feeds back into the initial setup and drives the structural wrinkling within the membranes. **Fig. 6.5** Yin Gao, Chao Gao, Jin Huang, 'MutateBrane': Distribution of spatial components based on fractal algorithm. The occupyable spaces unfold around a

hybrid structural system that gradually morphs from a compression structure in the core and plinth into smaller, tensile elements performing as building envelope. **Fig. 6.6** Yin Gao, Chao Gao, Jin Huang, 'MutateBrane': Bird's eye of the proposed installation (physical model/ stereolithography). **Fig. 6.7** Yin Gao, Chao Gao, Jin Huang, 'MutateBrane': Entrance to the public plaza (physical model/ stereolithography).

6.3

6.4

6.5

6.6

6.7

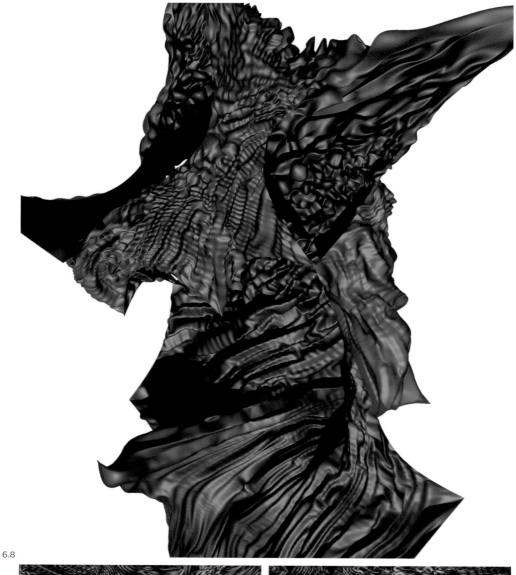

6.8

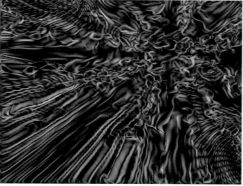

6.9

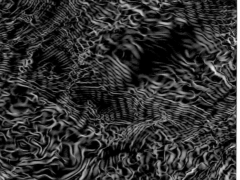

6.10

Fig. 6.8 Yin Gao, Chao Gao, Jin Huang, 'MutateBrane': Digital cloth simulation. Study of texture driven wrinkles within the membrane. **Fig. 6.9 — 6.10** Yin Gao, Chao Gao, Jin Huang, 'MutateBrane': Development of custom maps used as drivers for the dynamic wrinkling process within membrane systems. **Fig. 6.11 — 6.14** Yin Gao, Chao Gao, Jin Huang, 'MutateBrane': Analogue computational models back up conclusions drawn from digital simulations (plaster infused cloth model). **Fig. 6.15 — 6.16** Yin Gao, Chao Gao, Jin Huang, 'MutateBrane': Analogue computational models back up conclusions drawn from digital simulations (large scale resin infused elastane mock-up).

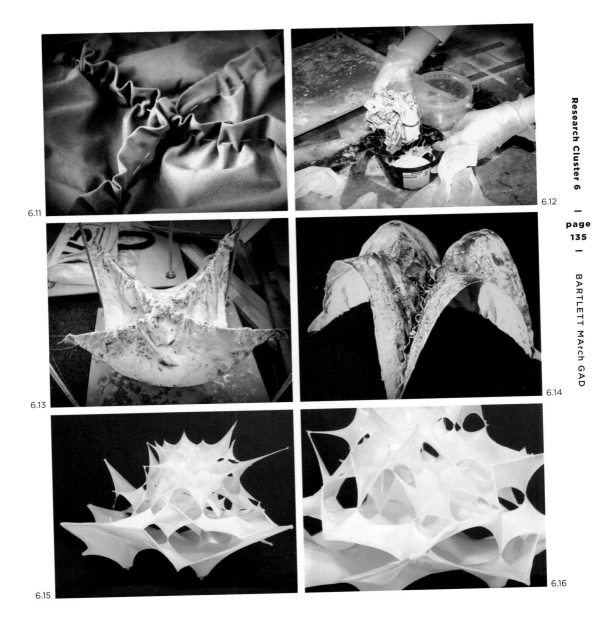

6.11

6.12

6.13

6.14

6.15

6.16

6.17

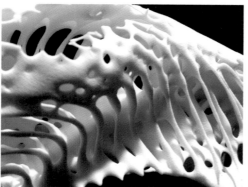

6.18

6.19

Fig. 6.17 Pinar Calisir, Maria Ines Gavelli, WeiWei Wei, 'SoundTransducer': Sound motion curves arrangement (physical model/ stereolithography). **Fig. 6.18** Pinar Calisir, Maria Ines Gavelli, WeiWei Wei, 'SoundTransducer': Individual sound motion curve, detail (physical model/ stereolithography). **Fig. 6.19** Pinar Calisir, Maria Ines Gavelli, WeiWei Wei, 'SoundTransducer': Digitalisation of Cymatics experiments with non-Newtonian fluid. The sound force exerting on the digital matter creates intriguing sequences of voids and interconnected spaces (physical model/ stereolithography). **Fig. 6.20** Pinar Calisir, Maria Ines Gavelli, WeiWei Wei, 'SoundTransducer': Particle field transformed by sound. Movement in time varies according to sound spectrum, scale and notations.

Fig. 6.21 Pinar Calisir, Maria Ines Gavelli, WeiWei Wei, 'SoundTransducer': Cymatics experimentation: Chladni Plate. Sonorous figures (salt on steel plate, 0.4 m x 0.4 m). **Fig. 6.22** Pinar Calisir, Maria Ines Gavelli, WeiWei Wei, 'SoundTransducer': Topological geometries generated through sound transmission. **Fig. 6.23** Pinar Calisir, Maria Ines Gavelli, WeiWei Wei, 'SoundTransducer': Interconnected nodes in a sound driven particle simulation.

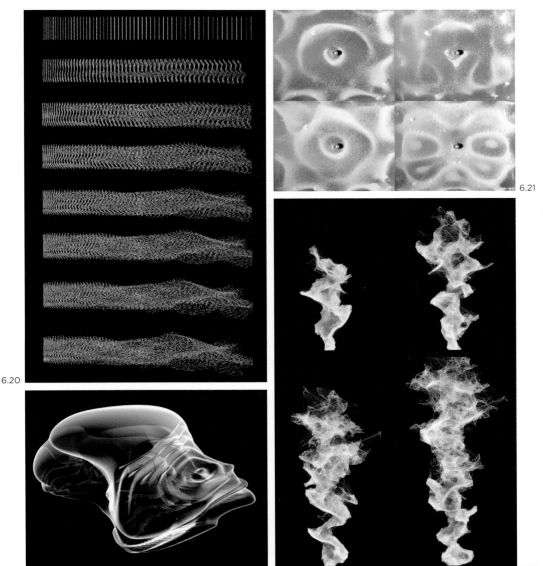

6.20

6.21

6.22

6.23

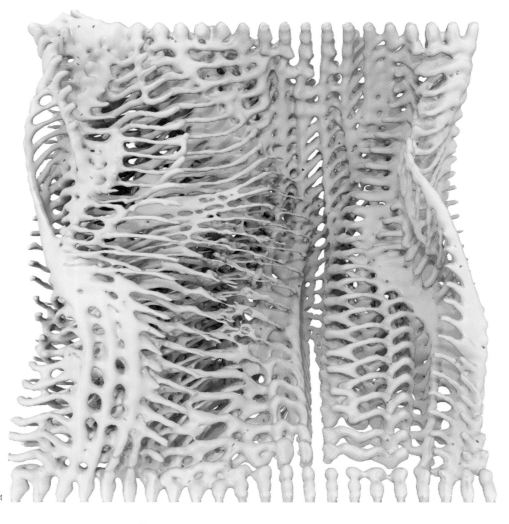

6.24

6.25

Fig. 6.24 Pinar Calisir, Maria Ines Gavelli, WeiWei Wei, 'SoundTransducer': Generative rib structure based on sound driven curve network. The movement created on the curves by sound intensity generates layering and different densities. **Fig. 6.25** Pinar Calisir, Maria Ines Gavelli, WeiWei Wei, 'SoundTransducer': West view of the architectural proposal in Limehouse, Tower Hamlets. The overall shape embodies the sound-wave form, of the environmental sound perceived by a person walking along a designed path on site. **Fig. 6.26** Pinar Calisir, Maria Ines Gavelli, WeiWei Wei, 'SoundTransducer': North view of the architectural proposal in Limehouse, Tower Hamlets. The structure unfolds on site, the volume and complexity correspond to the amount of sound mapped in the specific area. The structure grows in presence of higher sound values. **Fig. 6.27** Pinar Calisir, Maria Ines Gavelli, WeiWei Wei, 'SoundTransducer': Key view of the structure spanning over the railways. The variation of the form is reflecting the sound volume from the trains passing on the railways. **Fig. 6.28** Pinar Calisir, Maria Ines Gavelli, WeiWei Wei, 'SoundTransducer': Key view of the architectural proposal from Commercial Road. High traffic sound levels are translated into the form through the expansion of the structure. **Fig. 6.29** Pinar Calisir, Maria Ines Gavelli, WeiWei Wei, 'SoundTransducer': Transversal section. Wall, roof and floor are all blended together, giving a sense of continuous space. **Fig. 6.30** Pinar Calisir, Maria Ines Gavelli, WeiWei Wei, 'SoundTransducer': Structural ribs and skin, detail. Differentiation of surfaces and performance in presence of sound reflections, light and wind.

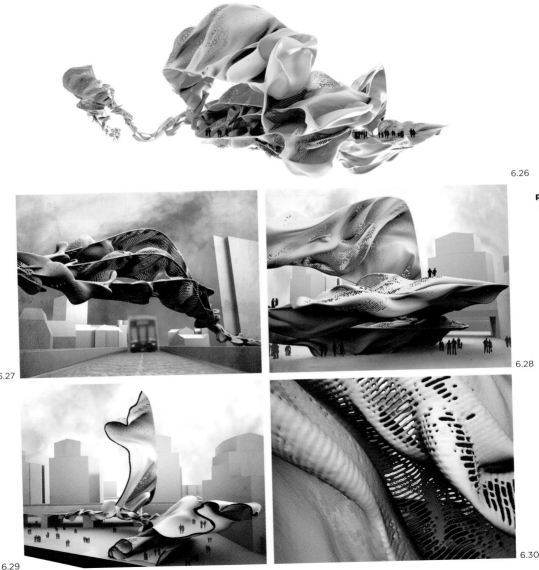

6.26

6.27

6.28

6.29

6.30

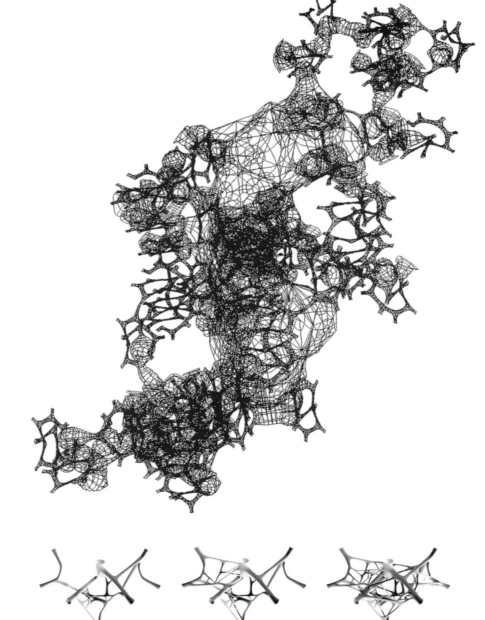

6.31

6.32

Fig. 6.31 Gopal Sankaranarayanan, Pegah Jalaly, Fatima Khatami, Anamaria-Beatrice Spulber, 'MindTheGap': Aggregation of cells gradually transforming from structural to spatial components. **Fig. 6.32** Pegah Jalaly, Fatima Khatami, Gopal Sankaranarayanan, Anamaria-Beatrice Spulber, 'MindTheGap': Structural component samples. **Fig. 6.33** Pegah Jalaly, Fatima Khatami, Gopal Sankaranarayanan, Anamaria-Beatrice Spulber, 'MindTheGap': Prototypical study of structure-to-space topology (largescale performative cardboard mockup). **Fig. 6.34** Pegah Jalaly, Fatima Khatami, Gopal Sankaranarayanan, Anamaria-Beatrice Spulber, 'MindTheGap': Assembly of structural cells (cardboard mockup). **Fig. 6.35** Pegah Jalaly, Fatima Khatami, Gopal Sankaranarayanan, Anamaria-Beatrice Spulber,

'MindTheGap': Close-up view of the proposed installation bridging between existing buildings at he prototype site in Earls Court Station (physical model/ stereolithography).

6.33

6.34

6.35

6.36

Fig. 6.36 Gopal Sankaranarayanan, Pegah Jalaly, Fatima Khatami, Anamaria-Beatrice Spulber, 'MindTheGap': Visualization of the architectural proposal within the existing urban fabric at the prototype site close to Earls Court Station. **Fig. 6.37** Pegah Jalaly, Fatima Khatami, Gopal Sankaranarayanan, Anamaria-Beatrice Spulber, 'MindTheGap': Customized form generation process using a combination of optimized path simulation and computational fluid dynamics. Building program and contextual information maps feed into the system. The resulting data cloud is used to propagate differentiated space filling components throughout the site. **Fig. 6.38** Pegah Jalaly, Fatima Khatami, Gopal Sankaranarayanan, Anamaria-Beatrice Spulber, 'MindTheGap': Topview rendering of architectural proposal occupying a voidscpace near Earls Court Station. **Fig. 6.39** Pegah Jalaly, Fatima Khatami, Gopal Sankaranarayanan, Anamaria-Beatrice Spulber, 'MindTheGap': Visualisation of the structure showing the gradual transformation from structural to habitable cells within the overall architectural proposal.

6.37

6.38

6.39

6.40

6.41

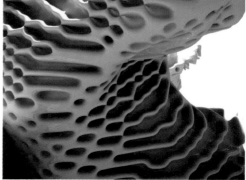

6.42

Fig. 6.40 Yuxiang Cao, Lisa Kinnerud, Fei Wang, Secil Zontur, 'Flow InForm': Initial form-finding; Wave generated structure, by reaction-diffusion processes. **Fig. 6.41** Yuxiang Cao, Lisa Kinnerud, Fei Wang, Secil Zontur, 'Flow InForm': Initial form-finding; Multiple fluid interactions. **Fig. 6.42** Yuxiang Cao, Lisa Kinnerud, Fei Wang, Secil Zontur, 'Flow InForm': Initial form-finding; Fluid based surface patterns. **Fig. 6.43** Yuxiang Cao, Lisa Kinnerud, Fei Wang, Secil Zontur, 'Flow InForm': Initial form-finding; Multiple fluid interactions and generation of turbulence bt material parameter variations. **Fig. 6.44** Yuxiang Cao, Lisa Kinnerud, Fei Wang, Secil Zontur, 'Flow InForm': Fluid simulation responding to existing fluid dynamical forces in the River Thames (prototype site: St Saviour's Dock). **Fig. 6.45** Yuxiang Cao, Lisa Kinnerud, Fei Wang, Secil Zontur, Flow InForm: Fluid attributes transformed to volumetric studies. **Fig. 6.46** Yuxiang Cao, Lisa Kinnerud, Fei Wang, Secil Zontur, 'Flow InForm': FowInForm: Building mass simulation informed by existing fluid dynamical forces, initial fluid simulations and volumetric studies.

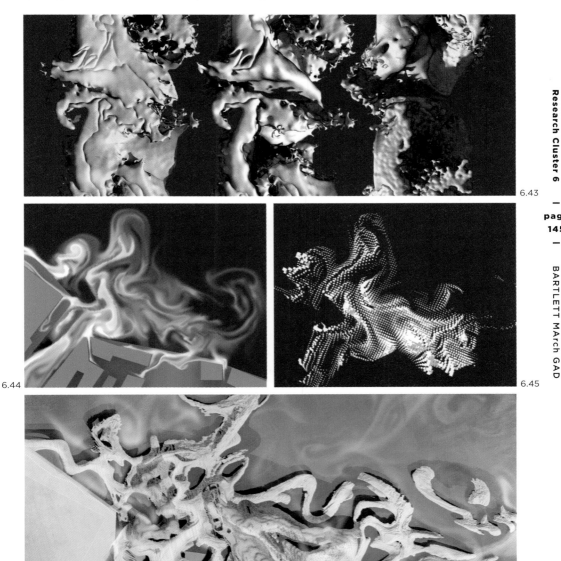

6.43

6.44

6.45

6.46

Fig. 6.47 Yuxiang Cao, Lisa Kinnerud, Fei Wang, Secil Zontur, 'Flow InForm': Main building massing with variations in surface porosity. **Fig. 6.48** Yuxiang Cao, Lisa Kinnerud, Fei Wang, Secil Zontur, 'Flow InForm': Driven by site specific fluid dynamical forces, environmental parameters and being subjected to certain spatial tasks, the natural and artificial construction of space can be synthesised. Perspective view of the connection between fluid formed buildings and landscape. **Fig. 6.49** Yuxiang Cao, Lisa Kinnerud, Fei Wang, Secil Zontur, 'Flow InForm': Perspective view, showing connectivity between the water, the fluid based urban landscape and the city. **Fig. 6.50** Yuxiang Cao, Lisa Kinnerud, Fei Wang, Secil Zontur, 'Flow InForm': Inner space with patterned surfaces. **Fig. 6.51** Yuxiang Cao, Lisa Kinnerud, Fei Wang, Secil Zontur,

'Flow InForm': Inner space with light transmitting surfaces. **Fig. 6.52** Yuxiang Cao, Lisa Kinnerud, Fei Wang, Secil Zontur, 'Flow InForm': Topview of architectural proposal. The tide influences spatial arrangements.

6.47

6.48

6.49

6.50

6.51

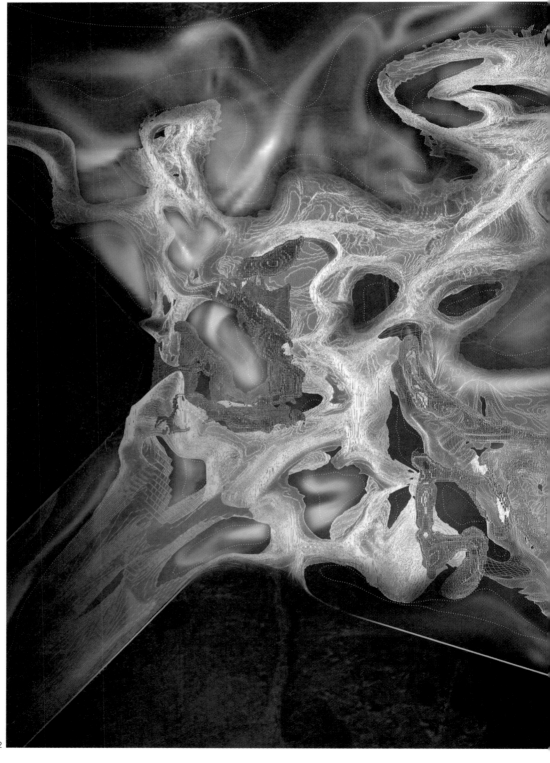

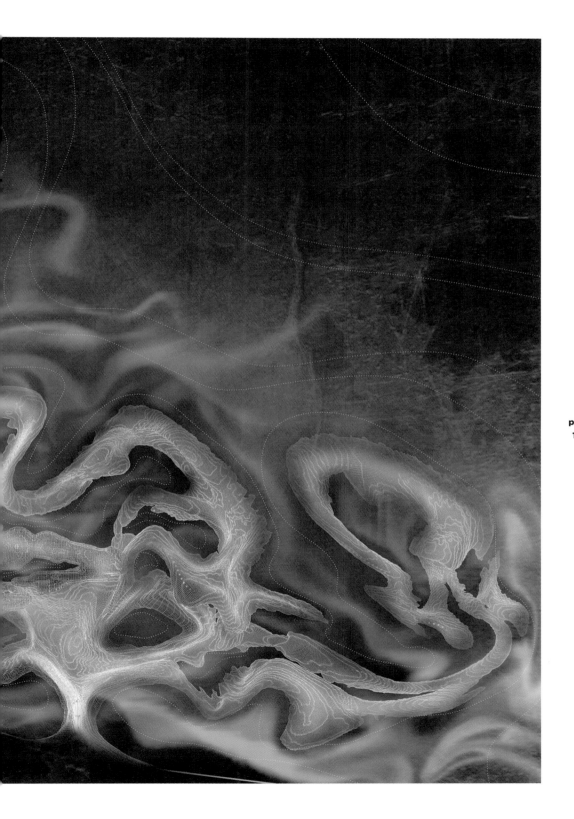

BARTLETT INTERNATIONAL LECTURE SERIES

BARTLETT PROGRAMMES

BARTLETT GENERAL STAFF

BARTLETT MArch GAD STAFF

BARTLETT FACILITIES

BARTLETT PROGRAMMES

The Bartlett School of Architecture offers a comprehensive range of architecture programmes, including courses directed at those seeking to become professional architects, as well as other programmes with specialisms in advanced architectural design, history & theory, and urban design.

PROFESSIONALLY ACCREDITED PROGRAMMES

BSc Architecture
(ARB/RIBA Part 1)
3 FT academic years of undergraduate studies

Year Out
1 year in practice

MArch Architecture (ARB/RIBA Part 2)
2 FT academic years of postgraduate studies

Certificate in Professional Practice
and Management in Architecture (ARB/RIBA Part 3)
6-12 months PT plus 24 months practical experience

NON-PROFESSIONALLY ACCREDITED COURSES

BSc Architectural Studies
3 FT academic years of undergraduate studies

Postgraduate Certificate in Advanced Architectural Research
3 months FT or up to 2 years PT of postgraduate studies

POST-PROFESSIONAL
MASTERS PROGRAMMES

MArch Graduate Architectural Design (GAD)
12 FT months of postgraduate studies

MArch Urban Design (UD)
12 FT months of postgraduate studies

MA History and Theory
12 FT months of postgraduate studies

MPhil/PhD
PROGRAMMES

MPhil/PhD Architectural Design
3 years FT or 6 years PT

MPhil/PhD Architectural History & Theory
3 years FT or 6 years PT

SHORT COURSES

Summer School
2 weeks in August

Summer Foundation
10 weeks from July to September

GENERAL STAFF

Bartlett Professor of Architecture

Professor Frédéric Migayrou
Chair

Director of School

Dr Marcos Cruz
Reader in Architecture

Professors & Directors

Professor Peter Bishop
Professor of Urban Design

Professor Iain Borden
Professor of Architecture
& Urban Culture,
Vice-Dean Communications,
Director of History & Theory

Professor Adrian Forty
MA Architectural History,
Programme Director,
Professor of
Architectural History

Professor Colin Fournier
Professor of Architecture
& Urban Planning

Professor Murray Fraser
Professor of Architecture
& Global Culture,
Vice-Dean of Research

Professor Stephen Gage
Professor of Innovative
Technology

Professor Christine Hawley
Professor of
Architectural Studies,
Director of Design

Professor Jonathan Hill
Professor of Architecture
& Visual Theory,
MPhil/PhD by Design,
Programme Director,
Director of Design

Professor CJ Lim
Professor of Architecture
& Cultural Design,
Vice-Dean International
Affairs, Director of
International Affairs

Professor Jane Rendell
Professor of Architecture
& Art

Professor Bob Sheil
Professor of Architecture and
Design Production, Director
of Technology and Computing

Laura Allen
Senior Lecturer, BSc
Architecture Programme
Director

Julia Backhaus
MArch Architecture
Programme Director

Dr Yeoryia Manolopoulou
Senior Lecturer,
Director of
Architectural Research

Dr Barbara Penner
Senior Lecturer, BSc
Architectural Studies Programme
Director, MPhil/PhD History &
Theory Programme Director

Frosso Pimenides
Senior Lecturer, BSc
Architecture Year 1 Director

Andrew Porter
MArch GAD Deputy
Programme Director

Dr Peg Rawes
Senior Lecturer,
Director of
Architectural Research

Susan Ware
Director of
Professional Studies,
Part 3 Programme Director,
Sub-Dean and Faculty Tutor

Patrick Weber
Senior Lecturer, BSc
Architecture Year 1 Director

Administration

General Administration:
Rachael Burnett
Michelle Bush
Emer Girling
Tom Mole
Luis Rego

Communications
And Website:
Jean Garrett
(Website)
Michelle Lukins
(PR & Publications)
Nadia O'Hare
(Communications)

Finance And Hr:
Carly Cunningham
Stoll Michael
Sheetal Saujani

Professional Studies:
Kim Macneill
Indigo Rohrer
Naz Siddique

Facilities:
Kevin Jones
John Riley
Dave Yates

DMC London, Media Hub,
Workshop, AV, Cadcam:
Abi Abdolwahabi
Martin Avery
Richard Beckett
Matt Bowles
Nick Browne
Bim Burton
Justin Goodyer
Richard Grimes
Simon Kennedy
Matthew Shaw
Paul Smoothy
Will Trossell
Emmanuel Vercruysse
Martin Watmough

BARTLETT SCHOOL OF ARCHITECTURE
MArch GAD STAFF

Professor
Frédéric Migayrou
Director

Andrew Porter
Deputy Director

RC1
Tutors:
Alisa Andrasek
Jose Sanchez

RC2
Tutors:
Dr Marjan Colletti
Guan Lee
Tea Lim

RC3
Tutors:
Professor Stephen Gage
Ruairi Glynn
Ollie Palmer

RC4
Tutors:
Xavier De Kestelier
Jethro Hon

RC5
Tutors:
Andrew Porter
Luke Pearson

RC6
Tutors:
Daniel Widrig
Fulvio Wirz

HISTORY & THEORY

Coordinator:
Professor Stephen Gage

RC1 Tutor:
David Andreen

RC2 Tutor:
Hannes Mayer

RC3 Tutor:
Sam McElhinney

RC4 Tutor:
Bruce Davison

RC5 Tutor:
Godofredo Pereira

RC6 Tutor:
David Scott

MArch GAD External Examiners

Professor Matias del Campo
DTMA — SIVA Fudan University,
SPAN Architecture & Design

Professor Evan Douglis
Rensselaer Polytechnic
Institute, Evan Douglis
Studio

Professor Kas Oosterhuis
TU Delft, ONL
[Oosterhuis_Lénárd]

Luca Galofaro
IaN+

MArch GAD Critics and Consultants

Pierandrea Agnius
Jeroen van Amejide
Paul Bavister
Shajay Bhooshan
Dr Thomas Bisbas
Dr Laurent Bozec
Edouard Cabay
Niccolo Casas
Angelos Chronis
Salmaan Craig
Miriam Dall'Igna
Bruce Davidson
Dave Di Duca
Christina Doumpioti
Steve Etienne

Pavlos Fereos
Nils Fischer
Paolo Flores
Irene Gallou
Pete Gunson
Fred Guttfield
Nahed Jawad
Yuting Jiang
Abdulmajid Karanouh
DaeWha Kang
Hanif Kara
Branko Kolarevic
Denis Lacej
Ilona Lenard
Ludovico Lombardi
Mark Miodownick
Phillipe Morel
Ed Moseley
Josef Musil
James O'Leary
Daniel Piker
Federico Rossi
Luis Miguel Samanez
Prasad Sawadkar
Patrick Schumacher
Irene Shamma
Harsh Tharpar
Emmanouil Vermisso
Matt Wade
Hugh Whitehead

GAD Workshops

Ezio Blasetti
Gregory Epps
Ruairi Glynn
Simon Kennedy
Skylar Tibbits

BARTLETT INTERNATIONAL LECTURE SERIES

Supported by the Fletcher Priest Trust.

The Bartlett International Lecture Series features speakers from across the world. Lectures in the series are open to the public and free to attend. Forthcoming lectures are publicised on the Bartlett Architecture Listing.

LECTURES THIS YEAR:

CJ LIM
ADRIAN LAHOUD
ALISA ANDRASEK
TOM WISCOMBE
MICHAEL HANSMEYER
CAMPO MANNINGER
RUY KLEIN
AKIHISA HIRATA
PHILIPPE MOREL
DANIEL WIDRIG
JOSEP MIAS
EZIO BLASETTI
MIKE WEBB
SKYLAR TIBBITS

PERRY HALL
DANIEL WIDRIG
SOU FUJIMOTO
CHRISTIAN KEREZ
ATELIER BOWWOW
FRANCK VARENNE
JAKOB MACFARLANE
PHILIP BEESLEY
PRESTON SCOTT COHEN
ROSI BRAIDOTTI
HITOSHI ABE
ED KELLER
BRANKO KOLAREVIC
PETER COOK

For more info see: Email: archlist@ucl.ac.uk
URL: http://www.bartlett.ucl.ac.uk/architecture/latest/events/lectures

BARTLETT FACILITIES

The Bartlett has extensive studios, workshops, seminar and lecture rooms, exhibition spaces, computing facilities and environmental laboratories. Specialist facilities in the School of Architecture include DMC London, Media Hub, an advanced computing cluster with printing/plotting and scanning (CADCAM) and an exceptional workshop.

MAIN WORKSHOP

The workshop, run by a team of craftsmen and architects, plays a crucial role in design education and research. The workshop contains a wide range of machinery for modeling wood plastic and metal.

CADCAM

The CADCAM workshop is run by a team of architects and technicians and plays a crucial role in the innovative teaching and research of digital fabrication. This facility includes one large CNC Router, two CNC milling machines, three laser cutters and one large-scale digital vacuum former.

DIGITAL MANUFACTURING CENTRE (DMC)

DMC London is the Bartlett School of Architecture's state-of-the-art digital manufacturing centre. The centre's advanced 3D modeling facility brings together a variety of technologies, including two ZCorp 3D printers, two Selective Laser Sintering (SLS) printers and one Objet Connex Multi-Material 3D Printer.

MEDIA HUB

The Media Hub is the central resource within the School for photography, audio visual, moving image and 3D scanning. The facility offers tuition in and access to equipment and techniques central to the production and representation of architectural ideas. Principle equipment and facilities include two wet darkrooms, one fully equipped lighting studio as well as 3D scanning support and 4D animation software.

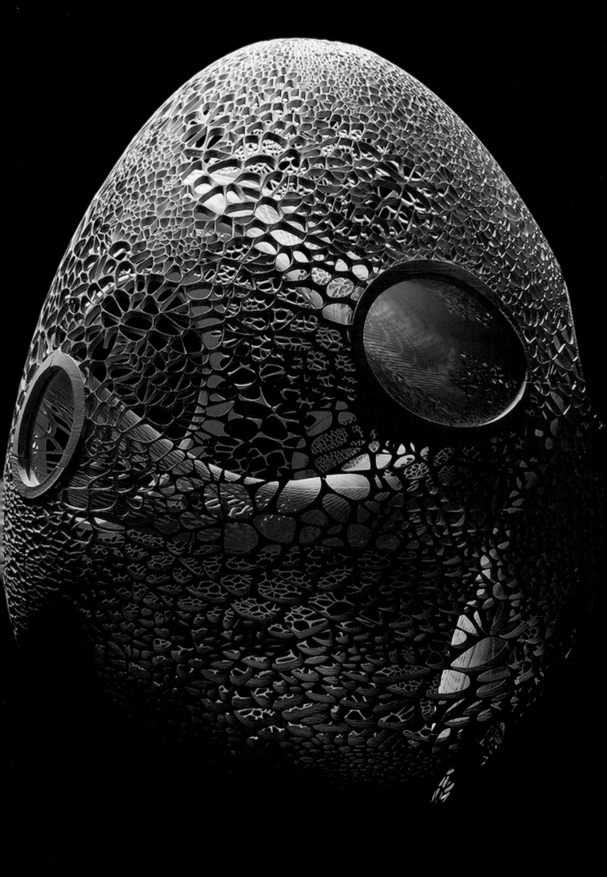

www.bartlett.ucl.ac.uk

PUBLISHER: Bartlett School of Architecture, UCL

EDITOR: Frédéric Migayrou, Marcos Cruz

ART DIRECTION & DESIGN: Johanna Bonnevier

EDITORIAL COORDINATION: Thomas Mole, Michelle Lukins

Printed in England by Quadracolor

ISBN 978-0-9572355-0-2

For more information on all the programmes and modules at
the UCL Bartlett Faculty of the Built Environment, please
visit www.bartlett.ucl.ac.uk

Bartlett School of Architecture, UCL
Wates House
22 Gordon Street
London
WC1H 0QB

T. +44 (0)20 7679 7504
F. +44 (0)20 7679 4831

architecture@ucl.ac.uk
www.bartlett.ucl.ac.uk
@BartlettArchUCL